THE HEALTHY MEDICAL CALL CENTER

60 PRESCRIPTIONS FOR LEADERSHIP, QUALITY, AND PATIENT SATISFACTION

CALL CENTER SUCCESS SERIES
BOOK 5

PETER LYLE DEHAAN

The Healthy Medical Call Center: 60 Prescriptions for Leadership, Quality, and Patient Satisfaction

© 2026 by Peter Lyle DeHaan

Book 5 of the Call Center Success Series

All rights reserved: No part of this book may be reproduced, disseminated, or transmitted in any form, by any means, or for any purpose, without the express written consent of the author or his legal representatives. The only exception is the cover image and short excerpts for reviews or academic research. For permissions: peterlyledehaan.com/contact.

Library of Congress Control Number: 2025923180

Published by Rock Rooster Books, Grand Rapids, Michigan

ISBNs:

- 979-8-88809-175-3 ebook
- 979-8-88809-176-0 paperback
- 979-8-88809-177-7 hardcover
- 979-8-88809-178-4 audiobook

Credits:

- Developmental editor: Julie Harbison
- Copyeditor: Robyn Mulder
- Cover design: Cassidy Wierks
- Author photo: Jordan Leigh Photography

To the healthcare heroes who serve out of view in medical call centers

Series by Peter Lyle DeHaan

Call Center Success Series: Join call center veteran Peter Lyle DeHaan, PhD, as he shares a lifetime of industry experience to help readers operate their contact centers with increased effectiveness, produce greater success, and generate long-term profitability.

Sticky Success Strategies Series: In the Sticky Success Strategies series of career development books, Peter Lyle DeHaan, PhD, breaks down key business strategies in a coherent, story-driven process to highlight what works and what doesn't. Through personal stories and eye-opening insights, he shares how readers can more effectively produce long-term results and increase their workplace fulfillment.

Be the first to hear about Peter's new books and receive updates at peterlyledehaan.com/newsletter.

CONTENTS

Let's Get Started 1

LEADERSHIP

1. Should You Switch Your Mindset from Calls to Contacts? 5
2. Channel Specialization versus Multichannel Proficiency 9
3. Customer Service Access Points 13
4. Orchestrating Change 15
5. Do You React to Today or Plan for Tomorrow? 17
6. Does Your Call Center Have a Fast-Food Hiring Mentality? 19
7. Pursuing Work-Life Balance in the Medical Call Center 21
8. What Message Does Your Call Center Send? 23
9. Coordinate with Marketing 25
10. Finish Each Year Strong 29

MANAGEMENT

11. Measure Success in Medical Call Centers 35
12. Evaluate Call Center Success 39
13. Empower Your Call Center Staff 41
14. Optimize Your Call Center Processes 43
15. Video Calls for the Medical Call Center 45
16. Make Sure Your Policies and Procedures Reflect Remote Work 49
17. Work-at-Home Option for Agents 51
18. Managing Home-Based Agents 53
19. Stop Reacting and Take Initiative 55
20. When Something Goes Viral 59

AGENTS

21. Celebrate Medical Call Center Agents 63
22. New Skills for Today's Agents 65
23. Agent Training and Development 67

24. Integrate Call Center Staff	69
25. Cross-Channel Strategies	73
26. Multichannel Scheduling	77
27. Reduce Agent Burnout	81
28. Create a Happy and Effective Workforce	85
29. Show Your Appreciation	89
30. Focus on the Good Calls	91
31. Be Thankful for Your Job	93

QUALITY

32. Providing Ongoing Skills Training	97
33. Provide Quality Service	101
34. The Quality Promise	103
35. Set Up a Quality Assurance Program	105
36. The Benefits of Outsourcing	109

PERSPECTIVE

37. Does Your Medical Call Center Need a New Name?	115
38. Do You Have a Mission Statement?	117
39. Embrace Your Stakeholders	119
40. Align with Your Organization	123
41. Integrate Your Call Center Operation	125
42. Build a Strong Team	127
43. Staff Is Key	131
44. Increase Your Call Center's Internal Visibility	135
45. Is Your Call Center Still Centralized?	137

PATIENTS

46. Improve the Patient Experience	143
47. Lessen Patient Frustration	147
48. Enhance Patient Satisfaction	149
49. Go Beyond the Call	153
50. Provide Multichannel Access	155
51. Tips to Deal with Angry Patients	159
52. Upsell Futility	163
53. An ER Visit Is More than Great Care	165

TOOLS

54. Key Reasons to Implement New Technology	169
55. Will Text Replace the Telephone?	171
56. Review Your Website	173
57. Do Video Calls Have a Place in Your Contact Center?	175
58. Integrate Your Call Center Tools	179
59. Multichannel Integration	183
60. Remote Patient Monitoring	187
Moving Forward	189
About Peter Lyle DeHaan	195
Books by Peter Lyle DeHaan	197

LET'S GET STARTED

The label of medical call center covers a broad range of understandings and implementations.

It might be a medical center help desk, a hospital switchboard, or a healthcare insurance company call center. It can also cover a telephone triage operation, a medical answering service, or a medical device manufacturer—as well as many other specialty areas.

Within this array are for-profit corporations and nonprofit enterprises. Some are outsourcing operations, while others are in-house initiatives.

This book has content for everyone involved with medical call centers. While not every chapter will apply in every situation, you'll find that most entries can be applied to your specific medical call center situation.

This book presents sixty topics, grouped into seven general categories:

1. **Leadership**: Look toward the future and plan for tomorrow.

2. **Management**: Oversee daily operations more effectively.
3. **Agents**: Focus on frontline staff, the cornerstone of the call center.
4. **Quality**: Seek to improve quality service.
5. **Perspective**: Sharpen call center outlook and mindset.
6. **Patients**: Have a patient-focused perspective.
7. **Tools**: Technology to help agents better serve patients and customers.

Each of the sixty chapters in this book ends with a medical call center prescription for your consideration.

With this structure in mind, read through this book as a guide to help you formulate ideas. Then use it later as a reference to focus on specific topics of interest. Refer back to the sections as needed for additional insight and reinforcement.

Let's begin.

LEADERSHIP

1. SHOULD YOU SWITCH YOUR MINDSET FROM CALLS TO CONTACTS?

THE ADVANCE OF CALL CENTER TECHNOLOGY

Over the decades, call center technology has advanced, customer expectations have expanded, and staffing practices have evolved. New service opportunities have emerged. The internet exploded into a global phenomenon that altered everything.

What hasn't changed much is the telephone. Call centers still answer calls, make calls, and transfer calls; you give and receive information over the phone. The telephone is the ubiquitous communication medium, and it is central to the call center.

During these years of technological transformation, there was also faxing and paging, but both were insignificant compared to the widespread practice of simply picking up the phone and calling someone to have a two-way conversation in real-time. Not too many people fax anymore, and it's been ages since I've seen a pager. Yet the telephone remains.

But now you also have email, text, and social media. Some call centers have fully embraced these technologies and integrated them into their operations. Others have persisted in focusing on phone calls.

Yet pressure exists for such centers to add these newer forms of communication and connection into their call center mix. As a result the *call* center becomes the *contact* center. To embrace this multichannel paradigm, your call center mindset must be about contacts, not calls.

Consider these forms of contact:

Calls: Phone calls represent the majority of contacts in almost every contact center. You excel at calls.

Fax: Some healthcare communication still occurs by fax. Though this channel is small, someone needs to oversee it. Why not the contact center?

Pager: Pagers have gone away in most industries, but they still have value in healthcare where reliability, speed, and disaster-adverseness are vital. Contact centers have always done a great job at sending pages, and some even manage pager inventory. There's no reason to stop now.

Email: Processing secure email is a natural fit for contact centers. You have the internet connection, the computers, and the staff. Your staff can send, receive, forward, and screen email, just as with calls.

Text: Texting is growing in most sectors. This is one more channel for the healthcare contact center to add to their arsenal.

Social Media: A growing preference for many people is to interact online with others through social media. Healthcare organizations require someone to monitor all those interactions, responding in a timely manner that is professional and accurate.

With the plethora of social media platforms, no organization can utilize them all, yet they must be where their patients are. The task of interacting with these social media-minded customers is ideal for contact centers.

Self-Service: A final consideration is self-service, the preferred option for many people when they have a question or problem. How, you may ask, does self-service become a contact center opportunity?

Doesn't self-service subtract from the contact center? Yes, every interaction handled via self-service is one less interaction handled by the contact center. Yet forward-thinking contact center leaders see two opportunities.

The first is that contact centers are in the best position to know what issues self-service should address. Poll a group of agents, and the top ten needs for self-service will quickly emerge. The contact center should serve as the advisor for self-service topics. Better yet, the contact center can take the lead role to produce and administer the self-service content.

The second opportunity is providing backup for self-service. Self-service cannot help everyone, every time. The contact center should catch those that self-service drops. As a bonus, these calls, taken in aggregate, then provide fodder for additional self-service content.

Call Center Rx: Whatever channels your contact center covers, keep in mind that it's not about the technology, it's about the contact.

2. CHANNEL SPECIALIZATION VERSUS MULTICHANNEL PROFICIENCY

EFFECTIVELY HANDLE COMMUNICATION CHANNELS IN A MEDICAL CONTACT CENTER

Having a multichannel operation means handling communications from various sources—or channels—such as text, email, and social media, in addition to the telephone. Let's look at multichannel from an agent and operational perspective, specifically comparing channel specialization with multichannel proficiency.

Ideally you want every agent trained and fully proficient to handle communication on any channel option that comes in, be it voice, text, email, video, social media, and so forth. Some agents relish being proficient on all channels, while others prefer to specialize. A contact center needs both types of agents.

Channel Specialization: An agent that specializes in one channel, for instance telephone calls, will develop a higher level of effectiveness by focusing on that one channel. Through repetition, they'll gain an enhanced level of skill through their specialization.

This will enable them to move from one call to another with greater speed and increased efficacy. In short, they'll get more done faster—and do it better.

But they must also be cross-trained on other channels. There are two reasons for this.

One is in the event of a telephone call that needs to switch channels, such as to move to video or email to better facilitate effective communication. In this instance you don't want an agent with a telephone channel specialization handing the call off to a video or email specialist. Instead, you want the original agent to move with the patient or caller to the new channel whenever possible.

The second reason you want agents cross-trained is so they can switch to a different channel if that channel's traffic picks up. Without this cross-training, you could end up with specialists in one channel sitting idle while specialists in another channel struggle to keep up.

Though you have agents that specialize in one channel and mostly work in that area, they must be ready and willing to jump to another channel when the situation requires it.

Multichannel Proficiency: Other agents would find channel specialization quite boring. They relish being proficient on many channels, even on every channel your healthcare contact center handles. They enjoy the variety that comes from interacting with patients on various channels. These multichannel agents can handle patient contacts from any source as needed, whenever needed.

This allows them to switch between real-time communication (telephone, text, and video calls) depending on the traffic demands at any moment. Yet at the same time they are equally proficient at processing non-real-time communication (email and social media) as required. This means they can effectively work in the channel where they're most needed.

Specialists and Generalists: While channel specialization is good for some agents and multichannel proficiency is ideal for others, this mix of channel focus is also essential for your contact center. Just like with healthcare, a contact center needs both specialists and generalists.

The specialists can concentrate on one channel, reaching a level of effectiveness that a generalist could never achieve. Yet a generalist is effective at quickly and easily migrating from one channel to another.

Though every agent in your contact center should be cross-trained to handle any channel, determine which area is the best for each agent, channel specialization or multichannel proficiency. You need both.

Call Center Rx: Strive to staff your multichannel contact center with both channel specialists and generalists.

3. CUSTOMER SERVICE ACCESS POINTS

ENHANCE PATIENT COMMUNICATION BY APPLYING CUSTOMER SERVICE SKILLS TO YOUR CALL CENTER

Customer service can occur at various touchpoints from the telephone, to online, to in person. Consider each one of these as it relates to your medical call center operation.

Telephone Access: The obvious and common source of interaction with patients and customers at medical call centers is the telephone. Telephone customer service skills are of paramount importance in this environment, as there is no face-to-face interaction, and everything relies on voice communication.

The need is to balance efficiency with effectiveness. Efficiency means to do things in the quickest, most cost-effective manner. Effectiveness means to address caller concerns correctly and to do so on the first call.

Another element of effectiveness is the caller's perspective. How do they feel about the call? Are they satisfied with the outcome? Did you leave them with a positive feeling or a negative one?

Online Access: As medical call centers expand their service connection points beyond the telephone, they embrace various online communication options. These include email, chat, and social media.

Each of these touchpoints provides an opportunity for customer service success or failure. Many of the skills required for telephone communications readily apply to online, but online channels require some additional skills.

These include typing speed and accuracy, being able to effectively multitask, and the ability to read and process typed communications quickly.

In-Person Access: At an initial consideration, face-to-face communication skills don't apply to call center situations. Yet as you integrate video into the call center, you add a new element to your communication skill set: the ability to incorporate body language into your communications.

This includes both what you see from the patient and what you visually supply to them. This opens another training opportunity you can use to enhance your call center agents' abilities to better interact with patients and callers.

Call Center Rx: Tap lessons from online and in-person communications to enhance your call center operation and boost agent effectiveness.

4. ORCHESTRATING CHANGE
WORK TOWARD ESTABLISHING A CHANGE-ORIENTED CULTURE

Change happens. And the rate of change is increasing. We experience change at home, in society, and at work in our medical call centers.

When considering change, there are three general truths. First, change is opposed. Next, change is viewed as loss. Third, change is mourned.

Each time you make a change—or attempt to make one—in your medical call center, you can expect to encounter these three normal change-resistant attitudes. Yet there is hope for a resolution.

Just as there are three barriers to change, there are three ways to help gain employee buy-in. Staff can more readily accept change if you embrace these three truths.

First, the change is incremental or small. Next, those affected by the change have a degree of input or control over it. Third, the change is clearly understood by all.

Here is how to best address change:

Communicate Often: The key to this is communication. Address change head on.

For every change, employees will wonder how it will affect them. Is their position in jeopardy? Might you cut their hours or change their shifts? Maybe they'll need to work harder. Perhaps you'll ask them to do something they find unpleasant. What happens if they can't learn the needed skills?

These are all worries about the unknown. As with most worries, few of them will ever occur, but with a lack of reliable information and leadership assurances, these irrational worries dominate everyone's thoughts.

Ongoing Reinforcement: Communication must also be ongoing; not just to key staff, but to all staff; not by one method, but many. This includes group meetings, internal blogs, memos, and one-on-one discussions. An open-door policy helps too.

Also critical is a positive, unwavering attitude from leadership. Celebrate milestones, thank the staff at each step, and provide rewards as needed.

A Change-Oriented Culture: Taking these steps sends a strong signal to the staff. Even though the change may still concern them, they'll take comfort knowing they have accurate information about what will likely happen. And with each successful change, the next one becomes easier to bring about.

You'll know you've created a change-friendly organization when your employees grow bored with the status quo and anticipate the next change. At this point, the potential of your call center balloons, your staff grows as individuals, and the future beckons. No one knows what that future will entail, only that things will change for the better.

So, sit back, and enjoy the ride as an instrument of change.

Call Center Rx: Guide your staff to embrace change and move toward establishing a change-oriented culture.

5. DO YOU REACT TO TODAY OR PLAN FOR TOMORROW?

HOW YOU HANDLE EACH DAY PREPARES YOU FOR THE NEXT ONE

In medical call centers, there's always more than enough to do to fill each day. Between staffing issues, patient or caller crises, and technical problems, there aren't enough hours to attend to them all. Given this pressure from the present, how can you ever prepare for the future?

Here are some thoughts about how to handle the workload at your medical call center.

Put Out Fires: The default mode of operation at most call centers is putting out fires. A problem arises, and you react. Sometimes multiple issues show up at once. Then you triage them and handle the most pressing one first, hoping you can get to the next one before it's too late. You do this from day to day, week to week, and month to month. It's all too easy for this approach to continue year after year. There must be a better way.

Be Strategic: Wouldn't it be better to control the day instead of letting the day control you? To do this, you need to plan. You must be strategic. This means you schedule your day, your week, and your month. You know what you will do each hour, and you don't let anything distract you from it.

Seek Balance: Of course, having a rigid plan is unrealistic.

Though this strategic approach deals with what's most important, it ignores the unexpected imperative issues that are bound to come up. If all you do is prepare for tomorrow, who will take care of today? That's where balance comes in. You need to balance putting out fires to being strategic, with reacting to being proactive.

To do this, make part of each day strategic and then allow the rest for reacting to the critical matters that inevitably crop up. This works best by blocking out an hour or two each day where interruptions are not allowed. Spend this time working on projects that will make your call center better. Focus on doing things today that will reduce the fires to put out tomorrow.

This is hard to do at first, but each time you're successful it brings you one step closer to running your call center better and doing it with less stress.

Call Center Rx: If you don't prepare for the future, the future will control you.

6. DOES YOUR CALL CENTER HAVE A FAST-FOOD HIRING MENTALITY?
SURVEY THE COMPETITION

When I worked as an industry consultant, one medical call center's staff kept complaining, "People working in fast food make more than we do." After hearing too many such complaints, I visited the seven quick-serve restaurants within walking distance of the call center. The staff was wrong, but the misinformation had gone unchallenged. After hearing the lie too often, the staff soon believed it as truth. My client had some work to do to correct this longstanding misinformation.

Too Much or Too Little? Compensation is a huge issue for call centers. Pay too little and turnover shoots up, training costs increase, and morale decreases.

Pay too much and expenses exceed income. No organization—including nonprofits—can remain viable if it loses money every month.

But what is an appropriate pay rate? Fortunately, the answer is close to home, back at your local fast-food restaurants.

Expectations: Not to disparage workers at quick-serve restaurants who fill a vital role, but if you hire agents at a fast-food wage, you'll get a fast-food mentality and a fast-food performance. Yes, you'll find the occasional star agent, but how long do you expect to retain him or her?

Generally, you find people with little work experience. They view the job as temporary, don't understand customer service, and fail to comprehend the necessity of being at work on time—much less giving two weeks' notice before quitting.

How Much More? To succeed, medical call centers must pay more than quick-serve restaurants, but how much more? Even fifty cents an hour can make a difference. But a dollar or two will have a much greater effect—if you do it right.

What you must avoid when raising your starting wage is to merely make it easier to find the same caliber of people. You must raise your standards too. When you pay more, you should expect more.

To determine the appropriate hourly rate for your call center agents you could pay someone thousands of dollars to do a wage study, or you could just visit your local quick-serve restaurants. Then distinguish your hourly rate and corresponding expectations from theirs.

Call Center Rx: Determine the appropriate hourly rate for your agents to distinguish your compensation and expectations from competing employers.

7. PURSUING WORK-LIFE BALANCE IN THE MEDICAL CALL CENTER
TAKE KEY STEPS TO REDUCE BURNOUT AND INCREASE RETENTION

We hear a lot about work-life balance. This is extra challenging in the healthcare industry, as well as with call center work. The intersection of these two areas results in a critical need to achieve a healthy work-life balance. Doing so will help reduce employee burnout and increase retention of both frontline staff and non-agent employees.

Consider these areas.

Nurses and Frontline Staff: Strive to provide a separation between work and nonwork activities for all agents. Employees in the office taking calls are working. Nonwork time is when they're not in the office taking calls. Don't intrude on their nonwork time.

This means not calling, texting, or emailing. Even if the interaction seems minimal, it sucks the employee back into a workplace mindset and distracts them from the nonwork activity they're immersed in. Great bosses don't do this.

Leadership and Administration: It's harder for people in key roles to not take their work home, be it mentally or physically. Yet when they do, it intrudes on their nonwork reality and threatens to unbalance their life.

Leaders, give supervisors and employees clear guidelines about when they should and shouldn't contact you when you're not in the office. Though you don't want to shut yourself off from essential communication, you also don't want to open yourself to around-the-clock interruption.

Two key steps to aid in this are empowering on-site supervisors and establishing on-call staff. When implemented properly, these two functions can help shield staff from work-related interruptions when they're not working.

Shift Supervision: Most call centers have shift supervisors. Train and empower them to make decisions on your behalf when you're not in the office. This covers the time when you aren't working and are attempting to enjoy the rest of your life.

You may worry about the possibility of shift supervisors making an error in judgment. It will happen, but don't view this as a mistake. Instead, consider it as a learning opportunity to equip them to perform their job with greater effectiveness.

On-Call Personnel: Some call centers have qualified staff rotate on-call responsibilities. In this way, the on-call person deals with all emergency and urgent situations that arise in the call center outside of regular business hours. In doing so, they shield all other staff from enduring work-related interruptions to their life.

Ideally, the on-site supervisors should be so well trained and fully empowered that they'll seldom need to contact the on-call person with a question or problem. This is how it should be, but for those exceptions, it's great to have a designated contact person to assist the shift supervisor.

Pursue an Equilibrium: Follow these steps to bring you and your staff closer to this important balance. When you do, you'll increase their job satisfaction, minimize the risk of burnout, and increase their tenure at your medical call center.

You'll realize these same benefits for yourself.

Call Center Rx: True work-life balance may be an illusion you'll never reach, but that doesn't mean you shouldn't try to get closer to it.

8. WHAT MESSAGE DOES YOUR CALL CENTER SEND?

IS SAYING "YOUR CALL IS IMPORTANT TO US" RHETORIC OR REALITY?

Whenever I call a company, I pay close attention to what happens. You probably do too. I look for specific details that thrill me. I also look for areas that need improvement. And I especially note my overall reaction to the call. Did they delight me, treat me with respect, and leave me with a satisfied feeling? Or did I feel frustrated over their indifferent attitude, poor response, and haste to move on to the next call?

Possible Caller Reactions: If I'm delighted, I look forward to my next call.

If I'm frustrated, I don't want to ever call again. I will do everything possible to avoid it.

Today's results foretell future interactions.

Mean What You Say: Every call center says, "Your call is important to us," but sometimes they don't act like it. When agents breathlessly rush from one call to the next, they send the opposite message: that each call is an interruption and a cause of irritation.

In the healthcare industry, call centers rise in importance as a key means to serve patients and enhance their overall level of care. While the call center can't replace in-person interaction with a trained healthcare professional, a good call center can certainly supplement it and serve as an invaluable resource to advance the overall level of care.

Put Patients First: This, of course, depends on call center agents delighting patients as they give focused, unhurried attention to callers. Agents must fully and professionally address the reason for the call. Yet a medical call center that leaves patients feeling frustrated hampers the overall provision of quality care and lessens the chance of the patient calling back the next time they have a need.

Make sure the phrase, "Your call is important to us," is more than a slogan or hollow promise. Their call is important to you. That's the message your call center wants to reinforce on every call. That's the way to make your operation be an indispensable part of the overall provision of healthcare in your community.

Call Center Rx: Show each caller just how important they are by how you treat them and how you serve them.

9. COORDINATE WITH MARKETING
THE CALL CENTER SHOULD BE THE FIRST TO KNOW, NOT THE LAST

Too many call center agents learn about the launch of their healthcare organization's product, incentive, or promotion from callers, not from leadership. I hope your operation is different, but I fear you, too, have found yourself in this unfortunate situation.

The results are dismayed callers shaking their heads in frustrated disbelief, flustered agents fumbling through the calls while irritation bubbles inside, and a peeved call center manager scrambling to piece together the details, while simultaneously trying to educate staff on how to respond.

Marketing doesn't intend to leave the call center out of the loop, yet it happens. And each time it occurs, a wall of distrust and animosity builds in the call center toward marketing.

And marketing—not knowing they dropped the ball—is angry at the call center for seemingly bungling their carefully constructed marketing initiative.

The solution is to coordinate with marketing.

Establish an Interdepartmental Connection: Though you may be upset with marketing for their latest oversight, don't take a confrontational approach. Instead adopt a cooperative mindset to seek your mutual benefit. Discuss ways to develop a standard communication channel.

One option might be a fixed, recurring meeting between marketing manager and call center manager, where the two sit down to talk about upcoming marketing projects. In doing so, the areas needing coordination will surface.

Another thought is for marketing to assign a call center liaison who has the responsibility to look at every marketing project for possible call center application, be it direct or ancillary. Then they can communicate needed details to the call center.

Also invite marketing to tour your call center—possibly even sitting with an agent to better understand the scope of their work. They will leave with a greater respect for the complexities of the call center, replacing a simple view of the job as "just talking on the phone—anyone can do that" with a more realistic appreciation.

Items to Consider: Sometimes your call center will be able to handle the work generated by a marketing campaign with no problem. Other instances—such as the new elements of the initiative or how to access an unfamiliar app or navigate a new database—will require training.

You may also need to adjust your call center schedule on launch day and thereafter. This could require overtime, scaling back on nonessential tasks for a few days, or even hiring more staff.

If you must hire staff for a marketing campaign but lack the needed time to fully train them, teach them only the skills needed for the marketing project, letting existing staff handle other communications. Then, once the campaign is over, consider completing their training for all other call types and communication needs. Also have a candid discussion with marketing about launch dates, addressing contingencies should a mail piece drop early or if delivery delays occur.

The result of following these recommendations is your call center and marketing working together for your organization's common good and your patients' welfare. And it all starts when you coordinate with marketing.

Call Center Rx: Strive to work with the marketing department, not in opposition.

[Discover additional insights in Peter Lyle DeHaan's book *Sticky Sales and Marketing*.]

10. FINISH EACH YEAR STRONG
HOW YOU CONCLUDE ONE YEAR PREPARES YOU FOR THE NEXT

How has this year been in your medical call center? I suspect you're ready for it to end. Though you may feel that way every year, the magnitude may be more pronounced this year. All the rapid changes and stressors in the healthcare industry pile additional burdens on the medical call centers that support them. Practitioners expect you to do more, and patients want you to do it better.

You're stuck in the middle. In addition, there are staffing issues, employee compensation expectations, and budget constraints. In situations like these, the tendency is often to merely hold on for the rest of the year and enjoy whatever holiday respite you can squeeze out. You won't think—or worry— about next year until that time comes.

But don't do this. Instead, do the opposite.

Strive to finish this year strong. Though you may feel like coasting, don't. Continue the momentum you have behind you to make the most of this year's remaining days. This will best set you up for success next year. Doesn't everyone want that?

Here are some ideas to help you finish this year strong:

Enjoy This Season: Though your work is important, it isn't everything. At least it shouldn't be. Take time to enjoy this holiday season in your nonwork moments. And whenever you have the opportunity, enjoy the holidays at work too.

Remember the adage about all work and no play. Don't be that person.

Thank Your Staff: Just because Thanksgiving has passed doesn't mean the time of being thankful is behind you. Take the time to thank your staff. Be intentional.

In a job that is short on appreciation and too often focused on criticism, a heartfelt thank you can go a long way to let your staff know you care.

Smile whenever you can. Do this even when you don't feel like it—especially if you don't feel like it. Smiles are contagious. Never forget that. Let your countenance communicate your thankfulness throughout the day, even when you don't say the words.

Celebrate Your Stakeholders: Remember why you do the work you do. It's to help others better address their healthcare needs and make their lives better. Without them you wouldn't have a job. Don't forget to celebrate them.

The patients and callers who contact you every day are your biggest group of stakeholders. Yes, they may be crabby at times and occasionally critical. But use this as a reminder to know how important the services you provide are to them and their lives. After all, if what you did for them didn't matter, they wouldn't care how you did it.

Your stakeholders also include your boss, your employer, and your organization—be it a for-profit business or a nonprofit entity. These are all stakeholders in your call center operation. Celebrate them, all of them.

Wrap Up What You Can: As you go about these initiatives, look at your project list. Surely you won't be able to finish them all this year but resist the urge to let them all carry forward to the next.

Each thing you can knock off this year is one less thing on your plate for the coming year. And won't that be a relief knowing that it won't be hanging over your head in the coming twelve months?

In considering this, remember to first enjoy the season. As you do, thank your staff, and celebrate your stakeholders. Then wrap up whatever pending projects you can so that they don't dog you into next year.

When you take these steps, you'll be poised to finish this year strong, paving the way for success next year.

Call Center Rx: Do what you can today to best prepare for tomorrow. Don't put off until next year what you can finish now.

[Discover additional leadership insights in Peter Lyle DeHaan's book *Sticky Leadership and Management*.]

MANAGEMENT

11. MEASURE SUCCESS IN MEDICAL CALL CENTERS
TOP METRICS FOR EVALUATING PERFORMANCE AND EFFICACY

Call centers have been around for decades, and the industry has an established set of proven metrics to measure overall performance and outcomes. Let's review some of these top call center metrics to use in measuring success. Then consider how they apply to non-call interactions too.

We'll look at three categories of metrics: patient centric, agent performance, and scheduling, with three key considerations in each category.

Patient-Centric Metrics

First Call Resolution (FCR): This measures the percentage of inquiries that are resolved on the first contact. No patient wants to call back, and no agent wants to receive those calls. Do it right the first time.

That's what matters most, especially in healthcare, where patient frustration levels are increasing and not decreasing. Now take this concept and apply it to all your other contact channels.

Abandonment Rate: Another patient-focused metric is abandonment rate. It looks at the percentage of callers who give up before speaking to an agent. They hang up in frustration because they waited longer than they expected to talk to an agent. A low abandonment rate signals better customer service performance.

Just as with FCR, give the same attention to your abandonment rate on your text channel and with any other real-time interactions.

Customer Satisfaction (CSAT): This seeks to quantify patients' overall satisfaction level after they interact with you. It can be measured through post-call surveys to assess the overall customer experience. This works equally well regardless of the communication channel used.

A key consideration, however, is to not ask too soon. For example, a CSAT survey tacked on to the end of a call often asks for feedback before the patient can give an informed answer. When this occurs, they'll guess or lie, but you'll never know.

Agent Performance Metrics

Average Handle Time (AHT): This measures the average time for an agent to handle a call, from start to finish. This includes agent talk time, hold time, and post-call work.

A low AHT suggests an efficient operation, but balance this with maintaining your patient-centric metrics, as a too low AHT will increase patient frustration.

Average Speed of Answer (ASA): This looks at the average time agents take to answer calls. A lower ASA reflects better call center efficiency and the likelihood of more satisfied callers.

Quality Assurance (QA): QA evaluations measure the quality of patient-agent interaction. This may be done by a person or automated through technology. Keep in mind that this occurs independent of the patient and merely addresses what the call center thinks is important to the patient.

Scheduling Metrics

Adherence: This metric confirms how well agents follow their schedule. Full adherence ensures agents are present when they're supposed to be.

Occupancy: Occupancy tracks the percentage of time agents spend handling calls and patient-related activities. It looks at work time versus idle time. Strive to keep agents comfortably busy without overwhelming them, which only leads to burnout. Yet not being busy enough leads to boredom.

Availability: This stat measures how much of the time agents are ready, or *available*, to interact with patients and callers. Agent availability is within the control of agents, determined by their willingness to be ready to communicate with patients.

To better measure call center performance, review these nine standard call center metrics and consider which ones you need to give more attention to. Then determine how to apply these concepts to all your communication channels.

Call Center Rx: Embrace call center metrics as a tool to help you manage more effectively.

12. EVALUATE CALL CENTER SUCCESS
KEY METRICS FOR EVALUATING AGENT PERFORMANCE

The impetus for call centers was to increase efficiency and save money. This was an admirable goal, and call centers did exactly that. The result is a model that most call centers operate under today. They use this in measuring call center success.

Yet efficiency often conflicts with effectiveness. This means that doing things faster and doing more of it may not be the right model for today's callers and patients.

The Old Model: With the multitude of statistics that call center platforms generate, it's easy to build a production-centric mindset based on efficiency statistics. Two common stats that call centers look at for agents is the number of calls answered and average call length.

These numbers get reported to agents. Staff quickly realize that the more calls they answer, the more they'll be rewarded, be it in praise or bonuses. They soon comprehend that the shorter they make their calls, the more calls they can answer.

The result is that agents drive themselves to do more and to do it faster. Management perpetuates this by rewarding that behavior.

When this happens, the call center is efficient and keeps costs low. The agents are happy because they're rewarded for accomplishing these results. But callers and patients lose in this scenario. It's no wonder that most all healthcare consumers dread calling their providers and the organizations that support them, such as insurance companies.

The New Model: Instead of letting efficiency dictate everything that happens to the call center, let's adopt a quality-first mindset. Address caller pain points. Put the patient first.

To do this, stop fixating on call center metrics such as number of calls answered and average call length. That doesn't mean to stop looking at them. It simply means to start deprioritizing them.

Instead, you need to look at other metrics that indicate quality, but standard call center platform statistics can't do that. Post-call surveys or some sort of patient feedback will be required.

This isn't as easy to gather and requires more effort to process, but it's what's essential to move past the negative reputation that medical call centers face. A key indicator to look at is customer satisfaction, sometimes called CSAT. It indicates how happy callers are with the responses they received from call center agents.

Related to this is FCR or First Call Resolution. Quite simply, did they accomplish the purpose of their call on one try?

Yes, there are times when two or more calls are required, such as when the patient needs to find information they don't have when they make their first call. But for the most part, one call should be all it takes.

Call Center Rx: To best evaluate call center success, stop focusing on speed and start focusing on quality.

13. EMPOWER YOUR CALL CENTER STAFF

ENSURE THE PROCEDURES YOU EXPECT YOUR EMPLOYEES TO FOLLOW STILL MAKE SENSE

A key approach to empower your staff is to eliminate processes that keep your call center staff from doing the job you hired them to do.

Many of the instructions you provide to your staff exist to address a past problem. Though some of these scenarios recur too often, other situations may have been an isolated instance that's unlikely to repeat.

Other expectations exist to accomplish management goals and advance operational paradigms. Though well intended and once applicable, their purpose may have lost relevancy over time. With this background in mind, let's reevaluate the procedures—that is, the rules—you've put into place for your staff.

Consider these actions:

Eliminate Obsolete Policies: Too many call center procedures once made sense but no longer do. You can make everyone's job easier by eliminating unnecessary rules. The fewer procedures you expect your staff to follow, the better they'll adhere to the ones that remain.

Simplify Existing Rules: Another category is procedures that have detailed and exacting expectations to follow. Although the general impetus behind the procedure still stands, you can look to lessen its severity. This could include reducing the number of steps required, removing time-consuming doublechecks, or empowering agents to act in specific situations without supervisor approval.

Implement Helpful Guidelines: Though your focus is on reduction, this doesn't mean all procedures are bad. In fact, you may need to add some.

Look for areas of ambiguity that your staff routinely struggles with. Could you ease their burden by giving them guidelines to follow? Would a straightforward framework save them the agony of trying to make a quick determination to address a perplexing scenario?

All call centers, especially those in the healthcare industry, require rules to run efficiently and effectively. But not all rules are good. You should eliminate some and simplify others. Also look to implement judicious rules that will help staff deal with challenging situations.

When you address these items, everyone benefits: you, your staff, your organization, and your callers.

Call Center Rx: Eliminate unneeded procedures and streamline rules to make your agents' jobs easier.

14. OPTIMIZE YOUR CALL CENTER PROCESSES
REMOVE WHAT'S UNNECESSARY AND RETAIN WHAT IS

Although I'm not trained as an industrial engineer, I think I'd make a good one. I have a knack for looking at processes and streamlining them. It gives me great satisfaction to take something overly complex and reduce it to its essential elements.

It doesn't matter what the task is, whether setting an appointment, doing a patient intake, or making a post discharge phone call, there's a process to assure it's done correctly.

Sometimes you view these steps as common sense and don't feel a need to document them—that is, until someone fails to follow what you think is common sense. Other times you establish procedures to correct past failures or streamline a confusing scenario.

Too often, however, these processes are more involved than they need to be. You need to look for ways to streamline them. Here are four considerations.

Remove Obsolete Elements: Any process that's been around for a while likely contains unnecessary steps. Though once required, they no longer are.

One medical call center I consulted with compiled data from every call for marketing, but marketing didn't even know the report existed. The person who requested it had left the organization two years before.

Eliminate Redundant Tasks: When I started *Medical Call Center News*, I entered data into three spreadsheets for each issue. Some numbers went on multiple sheets.

I reviewed the purpose I sought to accomplish and what I was doing. One section was a carryover from another publication and no longer applied. Another area contained information that was personally interesting but had no business relevance.

By taking away what was not essential, it was easy to see how the remaining data could smartly fit on one simplified spreadsheet. Not only did I save time with each issue, but the result was easier-to-use information.

A parallel issue that applies in many large organizations is multiple departments that want the same data. Enter it in one place and allow everyone to access it there. Don't do something twice when once will work.

Combine Steps: I once toured an apple farm and watched a man make cider using an old-fashioned apple press. Though I admired the employee's diligent work, the inefficiency appalled me. He could have combined five steps into two. And a simple adjustment to the press's set up would have eliminated all five, which took about 20 percent of the time to make each batch.

Cull Historical Baggage: Processes that have been around for a while often include steps that are there because of one error that happened long ago. Yes, mistakes do occur, but it's not wise to systematize preventing the possible reoccurrence of one long ago oversight.

Call Center Rx: Streamlining your processes saves time, reduces errors, and increases efficiency.

15. VIDEO CALLS FOR THE MEDICAL CALL CENTER
CONSIDER THE IMPACT ON AGENTS AND OPERATIONS

An intriguing call center technology is video. Consider the advantages of video calling.

Build Rapport: Most communication happens from body language, which puts call center agents at a definite disadvantage. All they can go on are the words spoken and the tone of voice. This is because phone calls miss the visual cues so critical in face-to-face communication, but video provides a fuller communication experience. This will help agents communicate more effectively and build rapport with callers and patients.

Aid Triage: In a telephone triage environment, video calls can pay off huge. No longer is the triage nurse limited to verbal interaction to decide on the best course of action. With video, healthcare practitioners can see the patient and incorporate important images and visual cues in their assessment. Not only will this make for more accurate results, but it will also get there faster.

Elevate the Call Center: For too many people, especially younger generations, the call center is low on their list of communication choices. Too many view a phone call as an option of last resort, while some dismiss it altogether. These same people, however, are open to video. Providing video as an option will draw some reluctant patients back to your call center. They'll consider it as a viable, and even preferred, option to find answers to questions and communicate with your organization.

Moving Forward

Where do you stand on video for your call center? Perhaps you've already embraced it. Or maybe you're moving in that direction by researching, planning, and even testing. Or are you doing nothing? This might be because you're too busy with other things, you worry about how your staff will react to video, or you need more technology to make it happen. But doing nothing is not a solution.

Take time to consider the role of video in your call center. To help you with this thought process, consider these elements and prepare accordingly:

Technology: Having the right video gear is critical to success. Don't select the cheapest option but pick the solution that provides great results. Just as you want your agents to have high-quality headsets, you should want high-quality video as well. Your reputation as a professional communications provider is at stake.

Environment: Look at your operations room. Specifically, what will be in the background of every shot? People walking behind agents as they talk with callers will be distracting. And if a broken chair, cluttered cubicle, or overflowing wastebasket is visible to callers, that sends the wrong message. You may need to install a backdrop for some agent stations. Don't neglect this with the intention to address it later. Fix it now.

Agent Appearance: In the audio-only world of a call center, an agent's voice is all that matters. In a video world, appearance is important too. And while an attractive visual helps a great deal, it isn't essential. But good grooming is. Many call centers already have a dress code in place. And if yours doesn't, this is a good reason to have one. But beyond attire there are basic personal appearance issues which you should insist upon for video success.

Training: Though some people are naturals, it takes practice for most agents to be comfortable in front of a camera, especially those who didn't grow up in a video-centric world where every action could be recorded.

In agent training, you tell them to smile because callers can hear the smile in their voice. With video, a smile is even more important because callers can see it too.

First, get your agents used to the camera being at their station before turning it on. Teach them how to use it and what to expect. Let them practice with coworkers. Only when they're ready should they begin sharing their video with callers.

Implementation: It's best to roll out a video initiative in phases. Don't announce that next Monday morning your call center will be 100 percent video enabled. You may suddenly find yourself short-staffed. Instead, phase in video.

Seek volunteers to pilot the program. Let the most eager ones go first. They can work out the bugs and help fine-tune your technology and processes. Building on this success, your cautious agents may begin to show interest. Work them into the schedule over time.

Then deal with the outliers. It might be that a few agents will refuse. Know what you will do if this occurs. There may be an ongoing non-video role for them in your call center. If that's okay, accept it. But do make sure all new hires are ready to embrace video.

Just as your callers will not all be ready for video at the same time, your agents don't have to be ready either. But you do want to be able to direct video calls to video agents and keep audio-only calls to audio-only agents.

Though no one knows how quickly the move to call center video will occur, it could happen sooner than we expect. Now is the time to begin moving toward that future.

Call Center Rx: Embrace—or at least consider—the value of video in your call center.

16. MAKE SURE YOUR POLICIES AND PROCEDURES REFLECT REMOTE WORK

UPDATE YOUR EMPLOYEE HANDBOOK OR DEPARTMENT MANUAL

When medical call centers scrambled to adjust to rapidly evolving health pandemic protocols to keep agents safe while continuing to work, the solution of many was to have agents work from home. Some call centers already had viable work-at-home protocols in place, and a few were already 100 percent remote, but most centers, however, had to execute a quick pivot to make working from home a viable reality.

Here are some considerations to better prepare for what the future may bring:

Align Policies with Practice: Having worked out the technological and logistical bugs of remotely answering phone calls from the security of a home office, take time to make sure your documentation matches reality and fully addresses the ramifications of people taking medical calls from home. Make sure your employee handbook, department manual, or written policies and procedures fully address staff who work remotely.

Prepare to Repeat: Even if home-based agents aren't part of your current call center operation, you may again find yourselves in a situation that requires working from home. In addition, even if working from a centralized location reemerges as a standard call center operating procedure, some employees will prefer to work remotely.

Make sure you have everything in place to allow them to remain in their home office. If you're unwilling to accommodate their request, you could find them leaving your organization to join one that will.

A New Normal: Having now experienced working from home, some call centers have embraced remote work as a preferable operational model. They've sent their employees home for good. Now they only need to make sure their internal documentation aligns with this new reality.

If you've experienced staff working from home, you already know what you must cover in your documentation. This will get you started. Next, check with an attorney to address legal concerns. Also consider contacting a consultant who is familiar with off-site employees working out of home-based offices.

With these documents in place, you'll find yourself ready to deal with whatever happens next.

Call Center Rx: Whether remote work is your new normal or a hoped-for one-time necessity, make sure your policies and procedures adequately cover it.

17. WORK-AT-HOME OPTION FOR AGENTS

CONSIDER THE PROS AND CONS OF HAVING REMOTE STAFF

Some medical call centers embrace the work-at-home option, while others categorically oppose it. Let's explore the pros and cons of using home-based agents, along with the potential risks of embracing or dismissing this option.

Benefits of Home-Based Agents: There are two primary reasons to use home-based agents to staff your medical call center. The main reason is to tap into a larger labor pool of qualified employees. This is especially critical given the nationwide shrinkage of credentialed healthcare workers.

A secondary reason is the potential to attract lower-cost personnel. This is because they live in areas with a lower cost of living. Though reducing labor costs should never be the driving force in pursuing work-at-home staff, it may be an exciting side benefit.

An ancillary consideration is being ready in the event of another pandemic lockdown that might prohibit agents from going to your office to work. You'll want to be ready if this happens.

Concerns About Home-Based Agents: Opponents to hiring work-at-home staff cite management challenges and HIPAA concerns. This is certainly understandable. Employees who are physically present are easier to oversee. When they work from home, who knows what they're doing?

Keep in mind that off-site call center workers have a level of supervision more comparable to most other healthcare workers. If this works in other scenarios, why not for your call center?

The Risk of Home-Based Agents: This concern over management brings up the risk of hiring work-at-home staff for your call center. Call center managers fear a HIPAA breach and PHI (Protected Health Information) being abused and misappropriated.

The key, however, is not a location but employee ethics. An unethical employee is just as likely to misuse PHI on-site as off-site. It's just that they must work harder to access and misuse the information if they're on-site. By the same logic, an ethical employee will treat PHI appropriately whether on-site or off. The fear over hiring off-site call center staff is understandable, but hiring the right staff negates this concern.

The Risk of Not Having Home-Based Agents: The chief risk of not using work-at-home agents is the risk of not being able to fully staff your call center. That's a disservice to callers and causes your existing staff to work even harder, which may result in burnout and resignations. Tapping home-based agents is a smart way to avoid this.

Call Center Rx: Look at the pros and cons to determine if having work-at-home agents is the right solution for your call center. Then factor in the risks.

18. MANAGING HOME-BASED AGENTS

OFF-SITE SUPERVISION IS DIFFERENT FROM ON-SITE

Many medical call centers are decentralized, linking multiple centers together and embracing home-based agents. While there are many advantages with home-based agents, the risks are great for those who rush into it without careful planning.

Here are some considerations:

Formulate a Clear Policy: Your call center either has agents who already work from home or agents who want to. Regardless, you need a clear policy to address this.

If agents working from home is something you will allow, specify how and when it can occur, what the expectations are, and how you'll measure agent efficacy, both qualitatively and quantitatively.

If you won't allow home-based agents, this also needs to be stated in writing.

A third option is whether telecommuting will be considered on a case-by-case basis.

Regardless, have a clear policy and stick with it. Don't subject employees to inconsistent behavior.

Have a Plan and Work the Plan: Once you have a plan for

home-based agents, clearly communicate it. Then carefully implement it.

A "plan as you go" approach will frustrate staff. Remember that whenever agents become unsure or upset, the best ones will leave first.

Train Managers to Properly Oversee Remote Staff: Many call center managers use the "management by walking around" style of overseeing staff. This common method is most effective when employees are centralized; it's disastrous in a distributed environment.

If a manager can't effectively handle remote staff, either provide the needed training or find a new manager. Don't make employees who work at home suffer because of ineffective management.

Avoid Saying Us and Them: Although usually not malicious, remote staff members are often overlooked. Imagine being off-site and receiving a message that there is a surprise in the break room or being told to check the Christmas exchange signup sheet posted next to the time clock.

When staff is physically separated, an "us versus them" mentality will emerge if left unchecked. Referring to remote staff as "them" and the local staff as "us," especially by management, is a staffing disaster waiting to erupt. Avoid it in all cases. Squelch it when it occurs.

There are many benefits from allowing agents to work from home, but if this is pursued without the proper preparation and forethought, all the anticipated advantages will evaporate. A bit of careful planning today will result in a better outcome tomorrow.

Call Center Rx: Successful management of remote workers requires a shift in perspective and practice.

19. STOP REACTING AND TAKE INITIATIVE
A BETTER TOMORROW BEGINS WITH INTENTIONAL EFFORT TODAY

Though I no longer work in a call center, I remember those days well. There was always something demanding my attention, some urgent matter to attend to. I'd often spend an entire day, sometimes all week, just putting out fires.

Charles Hummel called this the "tyranny of the urgent," where urgent matters occupy all our time and push aside doing those important things that matter more.

This is true in the call center industry and even more so when you connect healthcare to it. Do more, do it for less, and do it faster.

It seems there's always a pressing need that demands your immediate attention: an open shift, employee conflicts, or scheduling complications. There are also technical issues, vendor problems, and stakeholder complaints. It seems there's never enough time to handle everything, let alone attending to what's most important, such as making things better.

But working to make things better is exactly what you need to do. Here are some ideas:

Expand Agent Recruitment: A common call center complaint is not enough qualified applicants. Look at what you can do to change that. Is there a new labor market you can tap?

What can you do to make your call center more attractive to the type of people you want to hire? Addressing this will require some creativity. It may help to seek assistance from knowledgeable people outside your organization and even outside medical call centers.

Improve Employee Screening: Another frequent call center issue is agent turnover. You hire promising individuals, spend time and money to train them, and then they quit.

Look at why they leave. Also consider those who stay. Seek to find patterns. Then apply these conclusions to your hiring practices. But unless you can validate these findings, from a legal standpoint, you must be careful in how you use this information.

Enhance Training: A third concern is training, a task that is necessary, time-consuming, and expensive. Rethink how you train. Focus on what will make it more effective.

Ask around and see what others are doing, both those at other medical call centers, as well as those outside the industry. Every organization needs to train employees. Learn what you can from others and apply it to your situation.

Seek to make training fun, effective, and fast.

Expand Service Offerings: The idea of adding more to your workload may seem crazy, but often doing new things will invigorate staff. Look for additional ways to help patients and callers. This will increase your operation's value and serve people more fully.

Investigate New Technology: Technological opportunities for medical call centers change fast. It seems each week there's something new, something better, something more powerful that could help your staff do their job more effectively. Seek these tools. Test them and implement them. Your staff will thank you.

Don't try to address all these opportunities at once. That will drive you crazy. Instead, pick the one that will have the greatest impact on your operation and make it your priority. Let this become your important initiative that will take precedence over dealing exclusively with the urgency of day-to-day operations.

Call Center Rx: Pick one thing you can do now that will make the future better. Don't let the urgency of today keep you from addressing this important initiative.

20. WHEN SOMETHING GOES VIRAL
YOU CAN'T CONTROL WHAT HAPPENS ONLINE, BUT HOW YOU REACT IS KEY

Content posted on the internet can take on a life of its own, with the masses sharing it, adding comments, and promoting it to more people. This is usually an emotional response and seldom an informed decision.

The result is that something posted about you or your call center can go viral. There's nothing you can do about it. Yet you can determine how you respond. It's the one thing in your control.

Although we tend to think of something going viral as a negative occurrence, it can be positive. Don't lose sight of this. For positive viral content, enjoy it, add fuel to it, and ride it for as long as you can. The only challenge is knowing when the message has run its course. Then it's time for you to move on as well.

What's more common, unfortunately, is negative viral content. It's something you fear, but ignoring its potential to appear won't stop it. Instead, be prepared to react wisely to minimize its negative impact.

Here are some tips to dealing with negative viral content online:

Don't Go on the Offensive: A common response when attacked is to fight back. This seldom helps and often fuels the fire. Whoever first posted the information or was one of the first to promote it doesn't care about the truth. They care about attention and feed off it. The worst thing you can do is have a public conflict with this person. Their followers will defend them, and your followers will defend you. This escalates the situation and prolongs it.

Share Your Perspective Privately with Your Stakeholders: Quickly communicate the truth—or your side of the story—with your stakeholders. Keep your employees informed as well. A mailed letter may have the biggest impact and the least potential for misuse, though it also takes time to produce and deliver.

An email to your customer list is a faster approach. Just be aware that anyone who receives it can easily forward it or post its contents. Even when a supporter's actions are well-intended, it could make the problem worse. An email is especially risky if the message is hastily thrown together, has a critical tone, or is defensive.

You may consider posting something on your website but do so only after careful deliberation. It could hurt as much as it helps.

Let Your Supporters Defend You: Avoid the temptation to defend yourself online. Let your supporters do that for you. A carefully worded reaction from a third party could be the first step to vindicate you, lessen the negative impact, and give reasonable people a chance to consider your perspective.

Call Center Rx: You can't stop negative information from spreading over the internet, but you can mitigate its impact by forming a plan for how to best respond.

[Discover additional management insights in Peter Lyle DeHaan's book *Sticky Leadership and Management.*]

AGENTS

21. CELEBRATE MEDICAL CALL CENTER AGENTS
LOOK FOR WAYS TO APPLAUD CUSTOMER SERVICE AND PATIENT CARE EXCELLENCE

Working in a call center is challenging. Working in a medical call center is even harder. Throughout all the recent changes, the venerable call center agent adapts, presses through, and produces success in some of the most challenging situations. Here are areas where you can applaud the work of your medical call center agents.

Celebrate Customer Service Success: While some might see the job as a day-to-day grind or a never-ending repetition, astute agents will embrace their employment as a continual set of opportunities to provide customer service excellence. Acknowledge your agents with this attitude. Strive to catch them doing something right and celebrate their outstanding work. Do this in public and in private.

Celebrate Patient Care Excellence: Medical call center agents play a key—but frequently unrecognized—role in the patient-care continuum. They often stand as a patient's or future patient's first point of contact, smoothly ushering them into the organization's healthcare system.

Often agents serve critical functions throughout the provision of healthcare to maintain or facilitate forward progress for both patient and provider. And in growing instances, these same agents serve as a concluding point of contact as the patient wraps up a specific healthcare incident.

Your agents do this so often—providing critical links in the provision of patient care excellence—that they may not even realize it. Let them see the value they have in fulfilling your organization's goal of successfully providing healthcare services to your patients. Allow them to relish their role in your patient's health and in your organization's overall accomplishments. Know that this will encourage them in their too-often-underappreciated work.

Move Forward: Take time to celebrate your medical call center agents. Yes, you confirm your gratitude by providing paychecks and benefits. You thank them with your words. And you express your appreciation whenever possible. They deserve it.

Call Center Rx: Look for more ways to celebrate your agents' achievements and trumpet their accomplishments.

22. NEW SKILLS FOR TODAY'S AGENTS

HIRE STAFF WITH THE ABILITIES THAT TODAY'S CONSUMERS NEED AND EXPECT

There was a time when hiring managers looked for three key skills in their call center applicants: a pleasant and understandable telephone voice, good spelling, and neat penmanship. Yes, legible writing was key because everything was handwritten. Then computers arrived and the penmanship requirement was replaced with typing skills.

Today these three capabilities—voice, spelling, and typing—remain important, but you need to add more to your list:

Internet Awareness: You may assume that everyone today knows how to use the internet, navigate websites, and appropriately deal with problems that occur online. Yet you shouldn't assume this is the case. Instead, test applicants to verify this skill.

I recently talked to a rep who admitted to being confused in navigating her company's own website. As you can imagine, she wasn't able to help me.

Social Media Experience: In the same way, today's call center agents need to be comfortable using social media. Most applicants are, but don't assume this is always the case. Therefore, it's important to test them to make sure they have a working knowledge of the social media platforms your organization uses.

Even if their role won't directly involve communicating with patients and customers on social media, your staff should know how to navigate your social media pages. This way they'll be ready to assist your clientele if needed—and assume that at some point it will be needed.

Texting and Email Ability: Next, your agents need to know how to compose professional and comprehensible messages for text and email. Using slang and emojis may be fine in casual settings, but it has no place in the healthcare industry.

Agents must do well with spelling, grammar, and punctuation. Failure for them to have mastery over these skills will result in misunderstandings and reflect badly on you as a healthcare provider or support service. Test applicants to ensure their written communication will be an asset to your organization and not a detriment.

Video Ready: As discussed in the benefits and disadvantages of video calling, you need to hire staff with video in mind. Even if you don't currently use video in your operation, it's possible you soon will. Your employees need to be comfortable in front of a camera.

They must communicate effectively through their body language, in addition to the words they use and their tone. Though their words and tone are all they need when it comes to voice communication, video adds the nonverbal component, which is critical for effective communication to take place.

Hire staff that's video ready—and willing.

Agent Skill Essentials: In addition to hiring employees with a pleasant and understandable telephone voice, spelling proficiency, and typing accuracy, make sure they possess internet awareness, social media experience, texting and email ability, and are video ready.

This will provide you with a staff poised to help today's patients and contacts, as well as tomorrow's.

Call Center Rx: Hire staff with the skills needed for today and anticipated for tomorrow.

23. AGENT TRAINING AND DEVELOPMENT
INVEST IN YOUR CALL CENTER STAFF TO BEST SERVE YOUR PATIENTS

Call center agents are often the first contact someone has with your organization. If they conduct themselves well, this establishes a positive first step for a long-term successful relationship. But if they fall short, it may be your last interaction with that patient.

To produce successful call center outcomes, it's essential to train and develop your agents. Successful agent training will result in happier agents and happier callers. Given this, it's essential to emphasize agent training to help best serve your patients.

Communicate Expectations: Training begins with letting agents know what you want them to accomplish. Don't assume they know. Don't suppose they comprehend how to treat callers well or provide excellent customer service. Though they may, it's also possible they don't.

Therefore, clearly communicate your expectations as part of agent training. Tell them this at the beginning, remind them along the way, and retell them at the end. Make sure they don't lose sight of their fundamental objective as a call center agent at your organization.

Reinforce Fundamentals: Though some people are born

communicators, most are not. They need to learn the fundamentals. And they need to be reminded of what they've learned.

This starts with not being in a hurry when they answer the phone. Whenever a caller questions the name of the company they reached or who they're talking to, it signals a shortcoming on the part of the agent.

Listening is key. Agents should never presume a solution until they've heard everything the caller has to say. Yes, this may take a bit more time. But it also may save time overall.

Saying "please" and "thank you" is critical. These are common courtesies. So too is apologizing when appropriate. Sincerely saying "I'm sorry" covers many a miscommunication.

Following through on what an agent promised the caller or what needs to be done helps ensure first call resolution (FCR) and minimizes unneeded callbacks.

End each call with a memorable conclusion. Don't just hang up. The last thing an agent says is likely what the caller will remember. Make it a positive memory.

Teach Advanced Skills: After communicating expectations with your agents and equipping them with fundamental communication skills, now is the time to delve into advanced customer service practices. These include problem solving techniques, defusing tension, and communicating empathy.

Each of these can be a separate class, or even a series of classes. Introduce these advanced communication skills in your initial agent training but periodically build upon them to keep them in the forefront of your agent's day-to-day work.

Call Center Rx: When training agents, communicate expectations, reinforce fundamentals, and teach advanced customer service skills.

24. INTEGRATE CALL CENTER STAFF
PURSUE AGENT CROSS-TRAINING TO PRODUCE BETTER OUTCOMES AND IMPROVE EFFICACY

Cross-training improves efficiency, increases employee skills, and better serves patients. Cross-training also moves your operation closer to FCR (First Call Resolution), which produces both caller-centric benefits and improved operational outcomes.

There are two types of cross-training to consider: channel and contact type.

Channel Cross-Training: Many people use the phrase *call center*, but, as we mentioned, a better label is *contact center*. Various forms of contact arrive on different communication channels. The most common communication channel is voice, as in the telephone. It is ubiquitous and will continue to serve a vital role in your contact center.

Text emerges as another critical channel with increasing acceptance and use. Many customers persist in texting even when reverting to a phone call would more effectively meet their objective, both in terms of accuracy and timeliness.

Email communication is another channel. Some rely on it completely and expect contact centers to provide that option.

Social media is a fourth channel that is the default for some, even though it's not always ideal for healthcare scenarios. And there are other possible channels to consider as well.

The goal of channel cross-training is to have all agents adept at all channels. Though some may specialize, they need to know how all channels work and be able to use them. This allows you to integrate call center staff and have them move between channels as needed, either according to schedule or on demand.

Contact Type Cross-Training: The second type of cross-training relates to types of contacts. For example, an agent who focuses on taking messages should also be able to schedule an appointment or take a class registration. Or an agent who functions as a receptionist and spends all day transferring calls also needs training on other features to better meet caller needs.

Without cross-training, patients and callers can easily bounce around from one agent to another based on employee specialty and training particularity. With cross-training, however, one agent can address whatever need the caller may have. They could take a message for the doctor's office, register a patient for a class, and cancel an appointment, all before transferring them to a different department—assuming that's needed.

Contact type cross-training allows you to integrate call center staff more fully.

Contact Type Cross-Training Pitfalls: Not all cross-training is wise. Use common sense when you integrate call center staff. Though you don't want a highly paid nurse taking a message for billing, there's no harm in them doing so—upon occasion. Yet you don't want non-medically trained personnel addressing a patient's healthcare concern. This is a disservice to the patient, will likely provide misinformation, and could result in a lawsuit.

Therefore, encourage agents to have a patient-first perspective and seek to help callers in every way possible, while at the same time clearly knowing their limitations.

Embarking on an intentional and robust cross-training initiative will help you to fully integrate call center staff. The goal is that, within reason, any employee can help any caller on any request through any channel.

Call Center Rx: Cross-trained agents increase their value to your organization, patients and callers benefit, and contact center efficiency increases.

25. CROSS-CHANNEL STRATEGIES
CONSIDER THE OPTIMUM STRATEGY FOR YOUR CONTACT CENTER STAFF

At one time call centers handled calls and nothing else. They had one channel. That was it. Now many call centers handle more than just telephone calls. They've become multichannel. They're contact centers.

Along with phone calls—which is the predominant channel at many operations—we're now seeing text, web support, email response, and a multitude of social media platforms to monitor and engage. In addition to these is a possibility of handling two older channels: mail and fax.

Although there is overlap, each channel requires a separate set of skills, which means supplying channel-specific training. Do you want to cross-train all contact center agents so that any employee can handle any contact whenever needed, regardless of the channel? Perhaps you want specialists that excel in one area. Or is a mixture of both the ideal solution?

Here are some considerations about cross-channel training:

Channel Specialists: Contact center specialists, such as telephone agents or text representatives, handle communications through one channel and one channel only. Because they specialize in that channel, they excel at it and can serve customers with greater effectiveness, proficiency, and speed. A specialist will be more efficient in their channel than a generalist.

This is ideal for some operations, and it's ideal for some agents. These employees relish consistency and find comfort in knowing what they will do at work each day, each week, and each month. They counter the repetition of their work by embracing the unexpected variety from one interaction to the next.

For agents who like a variety of tasks, however, specializing in one channel is a horrific prospect. If you don't offer a way to counter their boredom, they'll leave as soon as a better-aligned job becomes available.

Channel Generalists: Contact center generalists relish the opportunity to learn and master each channel. They have a flexible mindset and see benefits of enjoying a varied workday. This means they need to know how to handle communication on each channel your operation offers. Give them cross-channel training.

Having a contact center staffed with generalists provides the most responsive configuration, with any agent able to handle any channel at any time.

This is ideal for time-critical communications that don't tolerate interaction delays, such as the telephone, text, and web support. (Having a delayed response with email, social media, mail, and fax isn't an issue, providing they're handled in a reasonable time.)

Selective Cross-Channel Training: The discussion between contact center specialists and generalists, however, isn't an exclusive one. You can have a mixture of both. You can even have partial cross-channel training, where an agent receives training on some channels but not all.

For agents who want to handle the same type of communication, let them specialize. Don't force them away from something they like into something they don't want to do. All that does is take a successful agent who happily serves you well in one channel and turns them into a disillusioned employee who longs for a different job.

Other agents, however, will clamor for the opportunity to receive training on and handle every communication channel you offer.

And they'll be the first in line to explore opportunities with new channels.

There's a middle ground, however, where agents may want to receive cross-channel training on specific channels with similar skill sets. One example might be the chat and email channels, which both need quick and accurate typing skills. But these agents may shudder at the idea of talking on the phone. Conversely, a phone agent may also enjoy text, as both have back-and-forth interaction with the contact.

In these cases, let agents select which channels they want to receive training on. Be sure, however, that cross-channel training is optional and not expected. Embrace those employees who want to remain one-channel experts.

Cross-Channel Implementation: Regardless of the degree of cross-channel training in your contact center, there are two implementation strategies for your cross-trained agents.

One possibility is with agents assigned to a particular channel for the day, with the understanding that you may reassign them to another channel as traffic warrants. This switch may be for an hour or two or for the rest of the day. Regardless, staff always begins the day on a scheduled channel.

The other approach is a universal distribution of contacts, with any customer communication going to any agent, regardless of the channel. This makes scheduling the easiest and offers the most responsiveness to customers, but it may come at a cost of the optimum efficiency that only specialists can achieve.

If your call center handles other communication channels, or is thinking about it, consider how you want to approach it. You can adopt a specialist mindset, pursue a generalist tactic, or embrace a mixture of the two.

Call Center Rx: Pursue the cross-channel training strategy that's ideal for your operation, your patients, and your staff. Balance their needs to provide the best outcome for all stakeholders.

26. MULTICHANNEL SCHEDULING
SCHEDULE AGENTS WITH THE RIGHT SKILLS TO WORK WHEN MOST NEEDED

You run a multichannel medical contact center and staff it with well-trained agents. Some specialize in one channel, others handle related channels, and some work on all.

This is a great start. Now comes implementation; now comes scheduling.

Schedule Channel-Specific Agents First: Start with the channel that receives the most interaction and schedule agents for that channel. Let's assume most of your contacts are via the telephone. Schedule telephone agents across your hours of operation to take a percentage of those calls.

If they can cover 50 percent of those calls overall, don't schedule them to cover 100 percent on some shifts and ignore others. Instead, populate your schedule so that your telephone-only specialists can cover 50 percent of those calls throughout your hours of operation.

Repeat this for your next highest used channel.

Continue this process for each channel that has enough traffic in any given time slot to call for scheduling a specialist to handle it.

As you work through this, you'll find a particular time-of-day or day-of-week that doesn't have enough traffic to keep one agent busy.

Don't schedule a specialist for those times. Instead, move them to an area with enough work to fill their scheduled hours.

Schedule Partially Cross-Trained Agents Next: With your single-channel specialists scheduled, next fold in those who are trained on more than one channel. Let's assume you have an agent trained to handle both text and email contacts. Place them on the schedule where there will be enough activity from one channel or the other to keep them busy.

Depending on traffic dynamics, they could spend their shift bouncing between the two channels or primarily receiving contacts on one channel or the other. This is to be expected, and they need to be aware it could happen. The key is to not schedule them for shifts where there isn't enough potential traffic in either of the channels they're trained for.

Schedule Fully Cross-Trained Agents Last: Once you have your channel-specific agents and partially cross-trained agents on the schedule, fill the remaining open slots with agents who are fully cross-trained to handle any channel. This is the last step of multichannel contact center scheduling.

Ideally you should have one fully cross-trained agent on every shift throughout the day. They'll serve as your buffer, able to pick up traffic from whatever channel has the greatest unmet need. Assuming you have enough staff, the fully cross-trained agents will smooth out your schedule. They'll pick up the slack on the channel where they're most needed.

You can use these fully cross-trained agents in two ways, and their personality may align with one approach or the other. Although able to take contacts on any channel, some agents will want to start on one channel and focus on those interactions until you move them to another—or until some preset condition exists, signaling them to make the switch themselves.

Other fully cross-trained agents are completely comfortable bouncing between channels from one contact to the next. They thrive on the moment-to-moment variability, which ideally positions them to pick up the moment-to-moment traffic changes that occur within any multichannel contact center.

Scheduling Tools: Knowing the philosophy of multichannel contact center scheduling forms the foundational understanding of what to do. Now comes the challenge of making it happen. For smaller operations with minimal channels, you can do this with some degree of proficiency on a spreadsheet.

A better solution, however, is scheduling software. But don't try to use a single-channel scheduling package. Instead, look for a solution that can take historical inputs from multiple channels and allow you to match agents according to the projected need.

Having a full-featured, robust scheduling solution will make the task of multichannel contact center scheduling much easier—once you've mastered the foundational staffing strategy.

Call Center Rx: Take a methodical approach to scheduling agents in a multichannel contact center.

27. REDUCE AGENT BURNOUT
CONSIDER A COUNTERINTUITIVE STRATEGY

The healthcare industry suffers from labor shortages, which contributes to burnout. This forces otherwise competent staff into exiting the industry. Though you won't solve this labor shortage dilemma, you can seek to minimize burnout of your essential medical call center agents.

Here are some tips to reduce agent burnout:

Consider Compensation: Though it's important to provide a competitive compensation package, increased pay is not a solution to burnout. Rather, it's a strategy to reduce turnover.

Offering to pay burnt-out agents more to keep them on the job will only serve to prolong their agony and damage your call center. They'll continue to work for the paycheck even though they can no longer do their best and may not even care.

Once you've ensured that you're providing the appropriate level of compensation, then turn your attention elsewhere to combat agent burnout.

Adjust Your Paradigms: When call centers are understaffed or receive more calls than projected, the default managerial response is to ask agents to do more. This includes having them stay late, work a double shift, and come in on their days off.

Though sometimes needed, this shouldn't be a prolonged scheduling strategy. Continually asking agents to do more will only push them into burnout faster.

Instead, at times you may need to take a debatable action. Let the calls pile up in queue instead of asking already tired agents to work more. Yes, having calls in queue will produce stress for the agents working and won't give callers the best level of service, but overall it will help protect your staff from burnout and therefore reduce turnover. It may be the best long-term solution.

Accept that you sometimes need to put your staff first over patients and callers.

Promote a Team Vision: We live in a society that celebrates the individual. Yet individualism is a lonely place to be. Recent polls, studies, and surveys confirm this.

What's better is community. Most people long to be part of something bigger than themselves. Your call center can serve in this capacity.

Deemphasize individual agent stats and metrics. Instead, focus on overall call center outcomes.

Celebrate Call Center Results: In a time when many criticize the healthcare industry, celebrate the ways your staff helps patients better navigate the system. This can range from getting a better appointment time all the way up to saving a life. Yes, it does occur.

Help each agent see how they can be part of making these things happen. Earning a paycheck—though necessary—is ancillary. Helping to improve people's lives matters more.

Acknowledge individual performance only when it contributes to the overall team success and achieves desirable outcomes.

Reduce Agent Burnout: Though it may not be possible to eliminate agent burnout, insightful call center managers can take steps to reduce its occurrence. Having appropriate compensation is a basic requirement.

Then follow three keys that should serve to reduce agent burnout. They are to adjust your paradigms, promote a team vision, and celebrate call center results.

Do these and you'll have happier agents who are less prone to burnout. They'll benefit. You'll benefit. And your patients will benefit.

Call Center Rx: Don't accept agent burnout as inevitable. Strive to combat it.

28. CREATE A HAPPY AND EFFECTIVE WORKFORCE
CRITICAL TIPS TO BETTER RETAIN STAFF AND SERVE PATIENTS

Operating a successful medical call center is hard. There is a never-ending tension to balance the expectations of patients with the needs of your staff, all the while remaining fiscally viable.

Implement the following tips to help produce a happy and effective workforce to keep your operation running smoothly and efficiently.

Compensation Package: I've never talked with anyone who thinks they're overpaid. And only a few people ever think they receive appropriate compensation. Most think they deserve more.

Ask any call center employee what's most important to them in their work and they'll likely say pay. They work to earn money so they can cover their needs and wants.

Though their actual paycheck is a big part of their compensation package, they're also looking for other benefits such as healthcare coverage and provisions for time off, including vacation, sick days, and personal time.

You could bust your budget trying to provide the compensation package your employees think they deserve, but you don't need to do this if you address other less tangible workplace related items.

Start by providing a competitive compensation package. Then implement the next five items to develop a happier and more effective workforce.

Managerial Support: Employees want to feel the support of their supervisors and managers. This starts with listening to what they say and showing them you care. Let them know you understand what it's like to answer phone calls all day long. You do know this, right? When they see you periodically sit down and take calls like the rest of them, it will do much to garner their attention and gain their respect.

Appreciation: Most managers say they appreciate their staff. But how often do they take time to tell their employees? How often do they do things to show it? This doesn't need to be anything expensive or spectacular.

I once had a boss who would look me in the eye each payday, hand me my paycheck, and say, "Thank you." He did this for every employee. Though I was too often frustrated with him in other areas, I had no doubt he appreciated me and my work.

Though this might be hard to implement if your call center operates 24/7, look for creative ways to produce the same results. And if your staff receives their pay and documentation electronically, seek other opportunities to make eye contact and give them a sincere thank you.

Scheduling: Appropriately staffing a call center is a tricky issue. You need to have the right number of people working to efficiently handle the communication that comes in.

If you don't have enough people present, those who are there will end their shift exhausted, frazzled, and frustrated. Yet if you have too many people working, your labor costs will escalate. Seek a scheduling balance that doesn't overwork your staff or tax your budget.

When developing a schedule, be considerate of the needs of your employees. If they rely on public transportation to get to work, don't schedule them on days or times when they'll have trouble getting to work or making it home. If they go to school, be sure to work around their class schedule.

Workload: Call center employees who move continuously from one call to the next throughout their entire shift are less likely—and less able—to give their best to every caller every time. They'll soon grow immune to the number of calls in queue and plod through their day from one call to the next.

Yet if they have too much idle time between calls, they'll become bored and their focus will wane. This doesn't provide good customer service either.

Instead, strive to develop a schedule that will give your call center staff a balanced workload that is just right, neither too busy nor too slow. It will make their shift go by quicker and produce better results.

Shared Vision: The final item, having a shared vision, is by no means the least important. In fact, when you and your staff share a compelling vision about what you're doing and want to accomplish, the first five points on this list aren't as important.

This doesn't mean you can ignore those items, but when you have a shared vision with your staff, they may be a bit more open to overlook shortcomings in other areas.

Call Center Rx: Strive to move closer to realizing a happier and more effective workforce.

29. SHOW YOUR APPRECIATION
TAKE TIME TO SAY THANK YOU

I've seldom been in a call center that wasn't busy. Even the ones that weren't quite as busy as others still had calls arrive at a steady pace. And this was during normal times. What about the not-so-normal times when things get busier?

Say Thank You: When call traffic spikes, agents committed to the work before them elevate their game to the next level. They shift into overdrive and handle more calls than they would on a regularly busy day. Be sure to thank them.

Celebrate Customer Service Distinction: But what happens when this spike in traffic isn't so much of a spike but more of a sustained onslaught of incoming calls, such as what might occur during a pandemic? This isn't a short-term situation which will get better in a couple hours . . . or tomorrow . . . or next week. This is a new normal that pushes you and your staff to the breaking point and sometimes beyond.

Although there's not much you can do to hold back the flood of calls coming in, you can let your staff know how much you appreciate their work. You can celebrate customer service distinction. You can recognize team members who serve patients with finesse. Take time to acknowledge their work and their dedication.

Catch Them Doing Something Right: This need not take a lot of time nor require much preparation. Just catch your staff doing something right and praise them—publicly, if possible. This will motivate them and encourage others. When you do this, be genuine. Make eye contact, state your appreciation, and thank them for their work. Then move on. Don't belabor it.

How long will this take? It might only require five seconds of your time. But the impact will last much longer.

These simple gestures show telephone agents that their work is noticed and appreciated, providing benefits that can't come from compensation alone. Unfortunately, when you're in the middle of a crisis, you easily forget to take the time to honor your staff for the exceptional work they do. So be sure not to overlook their hard work and dedication.

Call Center Rx: Look for ways to affirm your staff and the work they do.

30. FOCUS ON THE GOOD CALLS
DON'T FIXATE ON THE ANGRY MASSES

Working in a call center is challenging. Although it's been a long time since I answered calls in one, I'm still aware of how hard it is.

A Personal Story: Nowadays, I'm on the other end of the phone. In truth, I try to minimize my interaction with healthcare personnel, in large part because of the hassle that occurs once the appointment ends. I often spend much more time trying to get the bill paid than I spent talking to the healthcare professional in the first place.

Attempting to get my provider to work with my payor is challenging at best, and a futile endeavor at worse. Neither party will talk to each other, which means me talking to them separately. This requires me to phone their respective call centers. Then I ping-pong back and forth, working hard to reach a resolution but making little progress. Too often I get a different response each time I call.

Once I had two long-term outstanding medical invoices, which I'd been working on for several months. It would have been far simpler to ignore the negotiated fees and pay the billed amount in full, but because I had insurance, I figured I might as well try to use it. Right?

A call to my healthcare provider quickly escalated into a confrontation, with the agent threatening to turn me over to collections and me begging them to allow me to pay the negotiated fee as payment in full.

She would have none of it. I may have raised my voice. I may have said things I'm not proud of. I hung up with equal parts frustration and remorse.

A Chance for Correction: Three days later, I had new information. I called back for another round. I knew I'd reach a different rep because they're a large organization and I'd never talked to the same person twice.

Guess who answered the phone?

Yep, the same person I failed to treat with respect on my prior call. I groaned to myself. I sucked in a lungful of courage and opened my mouth. "Hi! I talked with you a few days ago and wasn't very nice. I'm sorry."

She didn't know what to say. Truly, she was speechless. After a silence long enough to make me wonder if I should apologize some more, she meekly said "Um . . . thank you."

Although we had a civil conversation this time, I got no closer to resolving this issue. But a week later, I received a letter confirming that the matter was closed; they must have accepted the negotiated fee as payment in full.

The Big Picture: Call center work is hard, especially when callers don't want to hear the information agents tell them. Difficult calls are common, so medical call center reps must take a small win whenever they can. Holding onto each small victory will help them weather the plethora of angry callers that are bound to follow.

Call Center Rx: To move forward with a positive attitude, remember the good calls and encouraging callers.

31. BE THANKFUL FOR YOUR JOB
DON'T FORGET THE GOOD PARTS OF OFTEN-CHALLENGING WORK

Have you ever left work and wished you didn't have to come back? Of course you have. Yet you return. Having this feeling means you care; it proves you're normal.

Working in a medical call center has its stresses, difficulties, and frustrations. Accept that you're bound to have bad days in your call center. That's expected. But don't let them obscure the good days and the good parts, for there are many.

Let's press pause for a moment and reflect on what you can be thankful for at your medical call center. Here are some ideas to get you started:

You Enjoy Financial Provision: At a basic level, we work to earn a living. Yes, every employee wishes they made more and thinks they should. But overall you're doing great. Your job covers your basic needs and then some.

Don't look at the 1 percent in the United States who have surpassed you. Consider the 99 percent in the rest of the world who wish they had your standard of living.

You Work with a Great Team: Every day you work alongside some amazing and talented people. Yes, there may be one or two who irritate you, but this is true in every job, as it is with every family and every social gathering.

Don't forget that you're part of a team that gets things done. Together you're stronger, more effective, and meet your mandate call after call.

You Help Others: Handling phone calls can have its drudgery. But remember that each caller is a real person who needs your support. They're calling you for assistance. And you're able to help.

Call after call, you help people. Because of you, their lives are a little bit healthier. You're doing your part to make the world a better place.

You Save Lives: Working in the medical call center can also have its life and death ramifications, especially if you're doing telephone triage. Though it may not happen every day, each life you save is a high reward that enables you to persevere.

Beyond saving lives, medical call center work also helps people emotionally or financially. Each call represents an opportunity for you to make a difference in that caller's life.

You Possess Purpose: Some jobs are boring, and others carry no meaning other than a paycheck. This is not so when you work in a medical call center. You have a purpose, a critical one. You and your coworkers help others on every phone call or contact. You save lives—whether literally or figuratively—on a regular basis.

Call Center Rx: Remember how much you have to be thankful for. You have a job that provides for you, benefits society, and carries significance.

[Discover additional related insights in Peter Lyle DeHaan's book *Sticky Customer Service.*]

QUALITY

32. PROVIDING ONGOING SKILLS TRAINING

TRAINING NEW HIRES IS JUST THE BEGINNING

Every new employee needs some training before they are ready to process calls at your call center. The length of training varies from one operation to the next, but the inescapable fact is that training must occur. But in too many cases, once this initial training is over, all intentional instruction stops.

Too many call centers fail to provide ongoing educational support for their staff.

The Need for Ongoing Training: Over time agent skills drift from what you expect and migrate toward what is expedient. Even more of a concern, they will learn from their coworkers sitting next to them. Though they may acquire some good skills this way, they're more apt to pick up less-than-ideal habits. It's a given that what you don't want to occur in your call center will much more readily permeate your entire staff than the best practices you desire them to emulate.

That's why it's essential to provide periodic training to your staff. Through this, you can reinforce the best skills in call handling, customer service, and patient satisfaction that you want them to consistently provide. Then you can teach them new, enhanced skills too.

Do this regularly for every frontline employee.

Though you may want to start with the under-performing staff first, this is backward. If you start with them, they'll view your training as punitive, which will detract from your objective of enhancing their skills.

Instead, consider starting with your best-performing staff. They are apt to view the advanced training as a reward, making them much more likely to retain and implement the customer service techniques you teach them. Then roll out the training to the rest of your staff. They'll receive your instruction more positively.

Here are some areas to consider.

Follow-Up Training: Telling someone how to do something once isn't enough. They won't retain much of it for the long term. The longer they work at your call center, the more bad habits they'll pick up—either from themselves or from their coworkers. They'll discover shortcuts that may appear to make their work easier but will end up circumventing the proper way you want them to do things.

That's why existing employees need to receive periodic reminders of how you want them to do their work. Without it, they're bound to veer from the path you put them on when you first trained them as a new hire.

Advanced Skills Education: After employees have learned the basics of processing phone calls and had some time to put their skills into practice in a real-world environment, now it's time to add to their skill set.

Teach them advanced customer service techniques that they can apply to their work. Even if you touched on these during their initial training, they lacked the framework to fully comprehend what you wanted them to learn.

Now that they have experience taking calls, they're ready to receive and implement more robust call-handling techniques. Once they see firsthand a need for these advanced skills, they'll be more likely to listen to your instruction and apply it to their work.

Technology Update Instruction: The final area for ongoing staff instruction relates to new and updated applications, software, and procedures. Don't implement an upgrade or change a process and expect your staff to figure it out on their own.

This wastes their time and increases their frustration level. It also disrespects callers. Instead, offer relevant instruction to agents before they encounter any technology change.

Make Ongoing Education a Mindset: Too many call centers view training as a once-and-done necessity. They can't figure out why experienced agents make basic mistakes, develop bad attitudes, or quit in frustration.

In many cases, being intentional about providing advanced training would have made the difference.

Call Center Rx: View training as an ongoing necessity.

33. PROVIDE QUALITY SERVICE
STRIVE TO PLEASE CALLERS

In addition to improving your call center by providing ongoing skills training, it's critical to provide quality service. Does your call center want to make callers and patients a priority? I expect it does.

But how do you know if you provide the quality service you talk about?

Quality Perception: I suspect the phrase *quality service* is in your mission or vision statement, or even on your bulletin board. But do you really provide quality customer service or just talk about it? Has quality service been mentioned so often that everyone falsely believes that quality service is a reality?

Most call center staff would say they provide great customer service, but the basis of this is their own opinion—after all, they work hard and do their best. (And if they don't work hard and do their best, why are they still working for you?)

Call Center Metrics: Many call centers try to measure quality using their system's reporting metrics, such as speed to answer, wait time, call length, and so forth. But these only consider things that management thinks reflect quality.

For me, I don't care if my wait time is six seconds or one minute, as long as the reason for my call is handled to my satisfaction. I don't care about *no transfer* initiatives. I'd rather talk to two people, and even re-explain my situation, if I can get a correct answer, as opposed to one rep who muddles through the call and leaves me confused.

Post-Call Evaluation: Other call centers do an automated, post-call survey, seeking answers to intangible issues based on callers' perceptions. This gets closer to identifying true quality, as it comes from the caller's perspective. Other methods are mail, email, and online surveys, as well as follow-up phone calls.

The Goal: Here's the main thing: If the caller is pleased, then quality service is likely a key reason why.

Customer service needs to be more than just a slogan. It needs to be a strategy, one that is fully implemented—and verifiable—with the callers' and patients' best interests in mind.

Call Center Rx: To address call center quality, strive to please callers. That's what matters most.

34. THE QUALITY PROMISE
ACTIONS VERSUS WORDS

Growing up, I heard a radio commercial with the tagline, "Service sold it." Even as a young child I grasped the concept that quality service was great for business.

Over the years, I've heard this concept repeated by various companies, including many call centers. Yet I give this grand platitude only passing consideration. The phrase now has a hollow ring; it seems a disingenuous assurance, holding an empty promise.

Good Ad Copy: What was once good business turned into good ad copy and now gets lost in the clutter of promotions we no longer believe. In fact, the louder companies trumpet this claim, the less credence I give it. I assume their quality is lousy, and their ad campaign's only goal is to convince us otherwise.

To paraphrase George Bernard Shaw, "He who can, does. He who cannot, talks about it." It seems too few organizations provide quality service anymore.

We all know someone who left one company because of poor quality and then subsequently left their competitor for the same reason. Eventually, having tried and rejected all available alternatives, they face the necessity of returning to a previously unsatisfactory provider. Their new goal is to pick the one who is least bad.

The Personal Touch: Does anyone provide quality service anymore? Fortunately, the answer is yes.

The key is the personal touch. For each positive experience I've had, it was always a person who made the difference. This was someone who genuinely cared and had a real interest in the outcome, someone who was willing to make me his or her priority and do what was required.

It's people who provide quality service. Give your agents the training, support, and encouragement to be those people. May your entire call center catch the vision and put it into practice on every call.

Key Questions: If your call center claims to offer quality service, is this reality or a hoped-for outcome? Do you provide a one-on-one connection with patients and callers? Does your staff provide the personal touch?

Can you honestly say, believe, and prove your call center provides quality service? If not, what changes do you need to make?

Call Center Rx: Prove your claims about quality service by doing it.

35. SET UP A QUALITY ASSURANCE PROGRAM
STRIVE TO ENHANCE CUSTOMER SERVICE TO BETTER MEET CALLER EXPECTATIONS

What does your medical call center do to improve quality interactions with your callers and patients? While some call centers have robust programs in place, others struggle with implementation or follow-through, and a few keep putting it off.

Regardless of where you stand on the quality continuum, too many call centers lack a methodical quality assurance (QA) program that they consistently use to track and improve the quality of the interactions their agents have with patients.

Here are some thoughts to move forward:

Start Small: Though you could begin with a grand comprehensive plan to have a dedicated QA leader or team evaluate every agent every day, this is too big of a vision for most organizations to start with. Instead, think small. Aim to evaluate each employee once a month. This feels manageable.

Though evaluating one call a month may not provide statistically meaningful insights, it does communicate to every employee the importance you place on the quality of their work. It also brings a customer service focus to the forefront of their thinking.

Be Consistent: Now that you've evaluated one call per agent in a month, repeat the process. Do it a second month and then a third.

Some employees will catch the vision right away, while others will have a wait-and-see attitude. But as you consistently assess one call per agent per month, your staff will see your commitment and take the goal of quality seriously.

Celebrate Wins: Instead of evaluating calls to discover where agents fall short, seek to catch them doing something right. Focus on the positive whenever possible. Yes, you must address some errors immediately, but even in this case, frame the shortcoming between what they did right.

Let them self-identify areas to improve. For example, listen to a call with them and ask, "What was good about this call?" You may need to prod a bit, provide suggestions, or offer affirmation.

After they've identified several areas of success, then ask them, "What is *one* thing that could've gone better?" Then offer instruction, encouragement, or support as needed to help them turn this one weak area into a strength.

Expand as Needed: Once you have a system down and have consistently evaluated one call per agent per month, look to expand your program. Seek to assess two calls per month. This will also be an ideal time to train other people in your QA process so that they, too, can help appraise calls. Continue to add calls to the process until you have a statistically significant dataset for each employee each month.

Also, be sure to allocate time for your QA manager or team so they can complete their call evaluation work. Don't expect them to squeeze this task in among many others. If you do, something will suffer, and I suspect it will be your QA program.

Consider Automation: With AI we have the potential to automate the QA process. Note that some offerings work better than others. Also expect *all* offerings to improve.

Regardless of the effectiveness of any automated—or semiautomated—QA program, don't remove human oversight. AI can make mistakes. It can proclaim a call as good when it is not. It can likewise mark a call as bad when it is good.

Call Center Rx: Implement a QA program to celebrate agent success, let them self-identify areas for improvement, and enhance customer service.

36. THE BENEFITS OF OUTSOURCING
CONSIDER SIGNIFICANT OUTCOMES, INCLUDING IMPROVED QUALITY

As healthcare facilities evaluate their effectiveness and efficiencies, they scrutinize every area. One such consideration is the call center. At some point they often consider the benefits of outsourcing their call center work—either in part or in full—to a specialist company that focuses entirely on providing call center and contact center services.

Consider these benefits of outsourcing call center work:

You Can Cut Costs: The top consideration when considering outsourcing is to save money. Reducing expenses is number one on the list of outsourcing benefits. The reason they can do the same work for less than many organizations can do in-house is that outsourcers enjoy an economy of scale. This allows them to be both efficient and effective to a degree that most in-house operations can't touch.

You Can Improve Quality: A common concern when considering call center outsourcing is the worry that quality will decrease. Though this could occur, it doesn't need to be the case and usually isn't.

Call center outsourcers do one thing, so they must do it well.

This is their focus. Quality is important to them. It's therefore reasonable to expect increased quality and enhanced patient satisfaction as another of the benefits of outsourcing.

You Can Free Up Space: Call centers use a lot of room. This is mostly for agents but also for support staff. In addition is space to house technology.

If you're running out of room for your call center, outsourcing all or some of the work is a smart way to respond without incurring a capital expense, which would happen if you expanded your call center facility.

You Can React to Labor Shortages: Call centers are also a labor-intensive endeavor. You need staff to run the call center. Qualified applicants are increasingly difficult to find in many areas of the country.

When you outsource your call center, you also outsource the labor component. The outsourcer handles staffing, and you don't have to.

You Can Allow for Better Focus: What is your healthcare organization's key competency? It probably isn't running a call center. As such, the call center can distract from work that matters more. Removing that distraction—or at least most of it—allows for better focus on what matters most to your organization.

The Benefits of Outsourcing: There are, of course, other benefits from outsourcing call center work, but these are some of the top ones.

When you outsource your call center to an outsourcing specialist, you can cut costs, improve quality, free up space, react to labor shortages, and allow for better focus.

Any one of these by itself may be enough to justify outsourcing. But expect outsourcing to address multiple pain points, perhaps all five.

Don't dismiss call center outsourcing over a preconceived notion. Instead, give it serious consideration.

Call Center Rx: Among the many benefits of outsourcing call center work is the potential to improve quality.

[Discover additional quality related insights in Peter Lyle DeHaan's book *Sticky Customer Service.*]

PERSPECTIVE

37. DOES YOUR MEDICAL CALL CENTER NEED A NEW NAME?
CONSIDER AN INTERNAL REBRANDING AS A STRATEGIC INITIATIVE

Functionally, you may label your operation as a medical call center, a healthcare contact center, or a medical answering service. This identifier may or may not be included in the name of your operation.

Regardless, it might be time to develop a new label. Though this could include a rebranding for marketing purposes, what I'm suggesting is rebranding yourself internally.

Rebranding Benefits: An internal rebranding accomplishes two things.

First, an internal rebranding allows you to refocus your attention on the work you do, the needs of your community, and your strategic plans. Each one of these initiatives must build upon a core framework of knowing who you are and what you do. Without first establishing this foundation, whatever house you build on it will not be stable.

Second, internal rebranding allows you to reposition your operation to the rest of your organization. Most people outside of call centers don't think highly of them. In too many instances this includes the rest of your organization: corporate, sales and marketing, accounting, tech support, and medical practitioners.

Few of them recognize the key role you and your staff play in facilitating healthcare-related communications between patients and providers. It's time to reposition yourself from a cost center to a central communications hub.

Of course, to have any significant impact, this internal rebranding must run parallel to a fresh attitude, an invigorated perspective, and an increase in professionalism in all that you do.

Rebranding Ideas: Don't let others look down on you because you're *just the call center*. Instead, reinvent yourself with a new label. To get your creativity flowing, here are some quick ideas to consider or build upon:

- Patient Support Center
- Healthcare Customer Service Center
- Patient Communication Hub
- Healthcare Information Center
- Patient Communication Solutions
- Healthcare Contact Center
- Medical Support Helpdesk
- Patient Assistance Center
- Telemedicine Support Hub
- Patient Contact Center

Cast a vision for what you want your operation to become and be known for. Move away from being *just the call center*, and embark on an internal rebranding effort to reposition your operation.

This will heighten your staff's self-esteem and enhance the rest of your organization's perception of you.

Call Center Rx: Having others view your call center differently starts with you. Rebrand your operation.

38. DO YOU HAVE A MISSION STATEMENT?

CREATE A VISION TO DIRECT WHAT YOU DO

Does your call center have a mission to guide all your center's work? If you don't have a mission statement, now is the time to develop one. Don't delay.

A practical mission statement will support and guide your staff. Don't let them flounder. Remember the proverb, "Where there is no vision, the people perish."

Mission Statement Questions: If you already have a mission statement, is it a hang-on-the-wall, feel-good, marketing-ploy type, or a succinct adage to guide employees?

Is it short enough for your staff to remember? Does everyone readily understand the statement? Does it serve as a framework to guide daily decisions and actions?

It should accomplish all three of these outcomes.

The Usual Approach: The conventional wisdom to create a mission statement is to make it a group activity, with input and review throughout the organization. This is to seek the buy-in of all stakeholders.

Yet, such mission statements become irrelevant over time. This is largely due to the turnover of the staff who were there when the statement was crafted. Then a new committee is formed with the mandate to develop a new one. This happens every few years, but this group approach is wrong.

A Better Way: Yes, you need staff support, but mission formation is a leadership issue. It must come from the top.

Then, communicate the mission statement regularly. Over time, staff will embrace and internalize the mission. It will guide their actions and their attitudes. This is as it should be.

Originating from leadership and reinforced by management, your mission statement will permeate your entire call center, directing action and guiding decisions.

Draft or update your call center's mission statement. Start today. Make it a priority. Your future may be at stake.

Call Center Rx: Draft or update your call center's mission statement.

39. EMBRACE YOUR STAKEHOLDERS
CONNECT WITH CRITICAL GROUPS WHO ARE OFTEN OVERLOOKED

When you embrace your call center stakeholders, this creates a better information flow between you and other groups that are often overlooked. Though they may seem ancillary to your call center, they're also integral to your success.

Here are some stakeholders to consider:

Vendors: First up for embracing stakeholders is your vendors and suppliers. They are critical to your call center success, so it's critical to have a good relationship with them. I've been on both sides of adversarial vendor-call center relationships, and the results are never good. For this reason, I always strive for mutually supportive, win-win interactions.

When you lift your vendors up, they'll lift you up. And if you tear your vendors down, you'll only hurt your operation as a result. Seek interactions and solutions that are in your mutual self-interest. Your positivity will be rewarded.

And when difficulties arise—which they invariably will—seek to work with your vendors to find a solution rather than harass or threaten them. Remember, patience needs to go both ways.

Investors: Whether you're part of a for-profit or nonprofit organization, someone invested money in your operation. They expect a return on that investment (ROI). No one wants to waste money.

If the call center fails to provide the return they expect, they'll close it down and outsource the work. In a worst-case scenario, the organization will go out of business and close their doors. Either way, all those call center jobs will be lost—including yours.

Yes, the owners of your operation control the purse strings. They are the ones who can say no to your funding requests. But they are not your enemy, so it's important to have a good working relationship with them.

Call center investors and owners are the second source of embracing stakeholders.

Staff: We've already talked about the importance of your staff, yet call center employees are also stakeholders. They can be appreciative of their employers or hostile toward them. While this is a choice they make, management plays a critical role in how well they buy into the mission and vision of the organization.

Key elements include their compensation package, managerial support, and how appreciated they feel for the work they do. Other areas are scheduling, workload, and a sense of a shared purpose.

If they're unhappy, they'll vent their frustrations with their coworkers, their families and friends, and potentially everyone who calls. Since they talk to a lot of people every day, one disgruntled telephone agent can harm your brand and hamper your objectives in quick order.

Thankfully, the opposite is also true. When they're treated right, they're much more apt to be happy and satisfied with their work. They'll likewise let other people know, and their work will show it.

When it comes to making your call center the best it can be, be sure to include your stakeholders and embrace them as part of your operation—and your success. Though these groups often go overlooked, they are critical to reaching your goals.

Call Center Rx: Look for ways to better embrace your stakeholders.

40. ALIGN WITH YOUR ORGANIZATION
DON'T STAY IN YOUR SILO OR FUNCTION IN ISOLATION

I once needed to call a company in the healthcare sector. With their initial call center I encountered long wait times, surly representatives, and little help in resolving my dilemma. I made multiple unsuccessful phone calls.

At last, one rep transferred me to a different area. My experience with that department's call center was the opposite of the first.

The employee answered quickly, was cheerful, and offered help. In one phone call, lasting but a couple of minutes, she resolved my concern. I thanked her for her helpful resolution and remarked how difficult it was to get to her department.

Her response took me aback.

"No one knows we exist," she laughed. "We're our company's best-kept secret."

It seems she worked in a silo within her organization. Her silo functioned wonderfully, in contrast to the organization's primary call center. What made the difference? I assume it started with management, but that's a different topic. Today's discussion is about aligning your call center with the rest of your organization.

Us Instead of Them: When you align with your organization you move away from the mindset of *us* referring to the call center and *them* referring to the rest of the organization.

Instead, everyone in the company becomes *us*.

Making this mental switch is key. Without it, any plans to align with your organization will not succeed. Embracing a holistic *us* mentality is the first step to successfully meld with your organization.

Focus on Others Instead of Self: As you make this mindset shift, you also shift your focus. By redefining *us* to include the entire organization, you encompass a greater set of employees who can band together to serve patients and callers.

Isn't serving why your organization exists? To help patients and callers? To best accomplish this, the focus must be on patients and what you can do—with your whole company behind you—to best address their concerns or needs.

A Team Approach: This reformed focus embraces a team approach to problem solving. The goal isn't to make yourself look good or even your whole department. The goal is to work as a team to make your organization shine. When you do this you and your company win, and—more importantly —so do your patients and callers.

Implementation: This grand vision to align with your organization is easier to visualize than to realize.

Though you can start it from within your call center, it will take time to permeate through your entire organization. It's easier when the initiative comes from the C-suite.

Of course, some managers will resist this change, but this reveals their selfishness and exposes their insecurity. They're more concerned about maintaining the status quo than about what's best for the organization and your patients. Don't be that type of manager.

Be a maker of change, not a roadblock.

Call Center Rx: Seek to align with your organization by working together for your patients' good and not in opposition to it.

41. INTEGRATE YOUR CALL CENTER OPERATION
FACILITATE BETTER COMMUNICATION WITHIN AND OUTSIDE YOUR OPERATION

With the staffing challenges that most every medical call center faces, it's more critical now than ever to optimize your operation for greater effectiveness and increased efficiency. One way to do this is to integrate your call center.

Let's consider some ways for enhanced contact center integration.

Integrate Your Staffing: Integrating your call center staffing is essentially a move from specialists to generalists. This means cross-training. It includes both cross-training on types of contacts (such as give information, transfer calls, take messages, schedule appointments, and so forth) and channels (such as phone, text, email, and social).

Granted, you may have some areas where cross-training doesn't make sense, but these should be exceptions and not the norm.

Cross-training improves operational efficiency, increases employee skill level, and better serves patients and callers. Cross-training also moves your operation closer to FCR (First Call Resolution), which produces both caller-focused and center-focused outcomes.

Integrate Your Tools: How often do your employees need to rekey information? Ideally the answer is never. Yet reality falls short of this goal. Not only is reentering data time-consuming, it's also error prone. And although a cut-and-paste transfer helps in both areas, it's more of a shortcut than a solution.

Related to this is integrating your auto-attendant with agent screens. Making an agent ask for information the caller has already shared electronically wastes agent time and infuriates callers.

The simple solution is to integrate your call center technology and smartly avoid this needless duplication.

Integrate with Your Organization: Next is to integrate your call center operation with other departments or divisions within your organization. Move from an us-versus-them mentality to a holistic we-and-us team approach. Seek proverbial win-win outcomes as opposed to clinging to a win-lose mindset.

This may be the most challenging integration initiative as it requires a shared perspective to reach a mutually beneficial result. Without having a common goal, the altruistic call center manager can fall victim to the me-first mentality of a predatory counterpart.

Integrate with Your Stakeholders: The next consideration is to integrate your call center with your stakeholders. For the in-house call center, this means a better information flow between you and other departments, such as marketing. For the outsourcing operation, this means a better data exchange between you and your clients.

Integrate with Your Staff: Don't overlook your staff. Seek to better integrate with them and their needs. Look at schedule development and posting, performance reviews, and handling the compensation aspects of their work.

This integration is even more critical now in the face of a worker shortage. Although your primary stakeholders are those you serve, without your staff you'd have no chance to serve them.

Call Center Rx: Pursue integration initiatives to make your call center operation more effective and be a nicer, saner place to work.

42. BUILD A STRONG TEAM
SUCCESSFUL OPERATIONS REQUIRE INTENTIONAL EFFORT

Most everyone who works in off-site customer service knows the importance of having a strong call center team. This is, perhaps, nowhere more important than in the healthcare industry. Though a committed crew is the outcome everyone desires, the path to get there is not always clear.

Here are five commonsense ideas to build a robust call center operation.

Provide a Professional Environment: It may come as a surprise, but building a strong team starts with the facility. If your operations room is dated, rundown, or has broken tools, you'll struggle to accomplish other improvements until you first resolve these issues.

Though people who work in a call center every day soon grow used to seeing its deficiencies, these are readily apparent to a new employee. Shield them from the negativity by fixing your facility's problems.

To do this, invite a trusted friend to tour your facility with a critical eye. Have them make a list of what needs to be taken care of. Fix what's broken. Replace what's obsolete. Make your operation room an attractive place to work.

Establish a Positive Atmosphere: With your environment updated, you've taken the first step in building a strong call center team. Now look at the intangibles. This means the overall atmosphere of your operation. Some might call it the vibe.

What vibe does your operation give off? If it's positive, expect positive results. If it's negative, brace for negative outcomes.

Turning a negative workplace into a positive place starts at the top. The director or operations manager must model positivity. Even when negative issues arise, address them with a positive attitude, all the while expecting improvement.

Encourage your middle management staff to do the same. You may have to politely correct negative attitudes, expressions, or expectations, but your management staff will eventually realize that you don't permit negativity.

Now repeat this with your front-line agents.

Though it will take time to turn a negative atmosphere into a positive one, you can do it; it's worth the effort.

Celebrate Success: Whenever success occurs for your call center, celebrate it. For big wins, consider throwing a party. For smaller wins, find a way to appropriately applaud it. These celebrations will encourage future successes.

In doing so, focus on group success, and only address individual accomplishments if the entire staff can receive it as a positive development. Otherwise, you're elevating one person at the expense of all others. Don't do that.

Encourage Initiative: With a professional environment and a positive atmosphere that celebrates success, now it's time to empower your staff to make decisions in your callers' best interests. This is the next step in building your team.

Yes, occasionally your staff will overreach, and you'll need to offer gentle correction. But never reprimand agents who do what they thought was the right thing for your customers. Most of the time their initiatives will be both well received by the caller and beneficial to your organization. That's the goal.

Provide Growth Potential: By the nature of its configuration, call centers offer very little growth opportunity for employees.

Nevertheless, look for every way possible to offer your staff opportunities. If you don't, your best employees will leave, while your marginal ones will stay.

The first thought for most managers is to think of promotions. While this is a sought-after outcome for many employees, it's not the only thing they desire. Other ideas include the chance to learn new skills, take on additional responsibilities, and share their knowledge with others, be it as a trainer, through a webinar, or by a lunch-and-learn scenario.

Get Started: Building a strong call center team begins with making a professional environment and establishing a positive atmosphere. Then celebrate success, encourage staff initiative, and provide growth potential.

When you persist in doing these things, you continually move your operation forward with an increasingly positive team attitude.

Call Center Rx: Strive to build a strong call center team.

43. STAFF IS KEY

TIPS TO HIRE AND RETAIN TOP TALENT

The key to success in any medical call center is people. Your staff is the backbone of your operation. But you know this. That's why it's essential to have a strong staff.

Here are some considerations to help you move toward this outcome.

More than Compensation: The first thing most managers consider when it comes to hiring and retaining staff is compensation. What you pay employees and the benefits you provide is critical to staffing success. But view this as a starting point and not the end.

If your compensation package is subpar, you place yourself at a severe disadvantage. Though you can overcome inadequate pay by excelling in the next three areas, you set before yourself a significant challenge to grapple with.

Instead, start with an adequate base pay and offer expected benefits. This is essential, but it's only the beginning. Don't assume you can hire and retain top talent merely by paying them more.

Physical Environment: Consider your facility. You've grown to accept your workplace as normal. It's comfortable in its own way, and you overlook its flaws. Instead, scrutinize it with fresh eyes, as a job candidate or new employee would.

Is it clean? Is it inviting? Does it convey a topnotch operation or something less than the best?

The physical environment in which your staff works establishes the baseline for how they conduct themselves and the work they do. If you expect the best from them, provide the best work setting. This is foundational if you want strong call center staff.

Culture and Mindset: Next, move your consideration from the physical environment of your facility to the attitudes and actions of your staff. What culture have you established? What is the prevailing mindset of your employees?

If they're discouraged and don't give their best, your new hires will follow their example. If your existing staff have negative mindsets and critical attitudes, expect your new hires to quickly adopt those as well.

Establishing a conducive culture and positive mindset among your staff starts with you. Model what you expect. Many will follow your example. Others may need your encouragement or require training.

Those who won't comply are your weak links. If they refuse to change their attitude, it's time for them to leave. Yes, you need to fire them. If you don't, you'll have no hope to build an accomplished team to serve your patients and callers.

Professional Interactions: Call center operations focus on quality. Most talk about having professional interactions and many pursue this goal. Yet professionalism isn't just reserved for the patients and prospects who contact you.

Professionalism extends to your staff too. Treat them with respect, and they're more likely to treat you the same way.

In this regard, the golden rule stands as an astute standard to follow: Do unto others as you would have them do unto you. This applies to everyone within your organization just as much as to everyone outside it, to those you're called to serve.

Let this goal start from the inside, and it will be more apt to spread outside.

Action Plan: To attract great staff for your medical call center, begin with your compensation plan. But this is just a starting point. Once you establish that foundation, build on it. Do this by providing a nice physical work environment, support it with a positive workplace culture and mindset, and cover everything with professional interactions with your entire staff.

When you pursue these objectives, you'll start to establish a commendable staff for your medical call center. This won't happen quickly, but remember that anything worthwhile takes time.

Call Center Rx: To get the best results, you need to start with the best staff.

44. INCREASE YOUR CALL CENTER'S INTERNAL VISIBILITY
IF YOU'RE NOT SEEN, YOU RISK BEING FORGOTTEN

Running a call center requires attending to many areas, such as staffing, quality service, and overall problem solving. Yet there is a political element too. It's being visible—in a positive way—to leadership.

Critical Questions: Does upper management consider your medical call center a profit center or a cost center? Are you under the control of another department, such as telecommunications, IT, or marketing?

Who does your call center director or operations manager report to? Does that person understand the critical role the call center plays in your organization? Do they comprehend your technological needs and the importance of a reliable infrastructure? Or is their primary concern that you don't make waves?

Regardless of how your call center fits into your organization, its place in the money stream, your department assignment, or the boss's affinity for your operation, there is a common need for ongoing, positive visibility.

Increased call center visibility is critical for two key areas. The first is budgeting; the second is your center's ongoing status and viability. Relating to both is staffing levels, technology upgrades, and additional software. And then there is respect.

Be Proactive: One option is to do nothing and hope for the best, which typically ends in frustration. The other option is to be proactive.

Does this mean making demands and becoming a general irritant to upper management? No. It means taking intentional steps to elevate your call center to earn the attention of key decision-makers.

Promotion Ideas: Look for ways that other people can do this for you. Seek others in your organization who will vouch for you and let everyone know the vital role you play.

Has your call center won any awards or garnered positive media attention? Has staff earned new certifications, received advanced training, or attended industry events? Have you, your staff, or your operation been awarded or recognized by your vendor? What about lifesaving phone calls? In this regard, a poignant patient testimonial can accomplish much.

Make sure upper management knows about all of these. Each time you remind them, it tips the balance in your favor. Take steps to improve your call center's internal profile today so you can enjoy the benefits tomorrow.

Call Center Rx: Increase the visibility of your call center within your organization. If you don't, you'll become invisible and soon be overlooked.

45. IS YOUR CALL CENTER STILL CENTRALIZED?
CONSIDER ALTERNATE STAFFING DEPLOYMENTS

In the early days of the industry, the label *call center* fit perfectly. You handled calls from a central location. This was necessitated by the platform you used, which was installed in your office. It consisted of physical hardware to switch calls and a local area network (LAN) for computers.

Centralized: The physical limitations of call center equipment required that all agent stations be on-site. It was impractical, if not impossible, to connect an off-site workstation. The result was everyone working as a team from a centralized operations room.

Though calls could originate from anywhere, they all went to one place. Your staff handled them with ease. It was efficient and easy to manage.

Multilocation: With technology advances, it became possible to connect a second location to the centralized telephone platform. Though the off-site agent experience was often not as fast or as reliable as its on-site counterpart, it did, nonetheless, allow for the first wave of decentralized call centers to occur.

This simple change, however, revealed some weaknesses in how you did business.

First, overseeing staff in two locations often required a different management style. By not being in two places at once, the manager tended to ignore staff at the other location. Though some employees worked well without direct in-person oversight, others did not. Too often quality struggled and productivity dropped.

The other issue was "out of sight, out of mind." Leaving a box of donuts in the break room dismisses employees at a second location. Also, the once-common practice of posting notices on a physical bulletin board ignores staff at the second site. And holding an office potluck becomes problematic, resulting in further division as opposed to enhancing camaraderie.

Too often, an us-versus-them mentality emerges between two sparring locations. Yet, over time, wise managers adjust their management style and operational practices to equally embrace employees at both locations.

Home Based: As hosted systems, also called SaaS (Software as a Service), became available, the longstanding dream of many a manager at last became a viable reality.

What was this grand vision? A truly distributed workforce where every employee could work at a different location, such as their own home. In truth, any location with a stable internet connection could become an effective remote-agent station.

Though some resisted this opportunity, citing HIPAA and data security concerns, others already had procedures in place to effectively deal with this. And when the pandemic hit, forcing many call centers to close or pivot, some easily switched to a 100 percent home-based operation, either as a short-term solution or as a permanent paradigm shift.

Hybrid: Though some call centers today operate solely in one of these three operational models, most take a hybrid approach.

In this decentralized model, some staff work in a central office, other employees operate from a second location, and some agents work from their home offices. This allows for the greatest efficiency and flexibility.

In this way, your operation benefits, your organization benefits, and your patients and callers benefit.

Call Center Rx: Increase call center work flexibility by decentralizing your agent deployment options.

PATIENTS

46. IMPROVE THE PATIENT EXPERIENCE
FOCUS ON WHAT YOU DO BASED ON WHAT MATTERS MOST TO YOUR PATIENTS

Call center platforms generate a myriad of statistics. The vast number of them is sure to overwhelm any manager, so you pick a few key ones to track. Common ones are average speed to answer, hold time, and abandonment rate.

We also look at first call resolution and customer satisfaction. Specific to healthcare, we may look at patient acquisition cost, appointment setting, and physician referrals.

Yet patients don't care about these numbers. They have different priorities. Therefore, the best way to improve patient experience in your medical call center is to focus on what matters most to them.

Provide Correct Answers: Your callers and your patients expect you to provide correct answers to their questions. Though this is of the utmost importance in a telephone triage setting—sometimes it is a matter of life and death—accuracy matters regardless of why they call.

Giving incorrect information will cause them to take wrong actions or make incorrect decisions. It may result in them calling again in hopes of talking with another agent to get a credible response. And they'll always be likely to share their frustration with other people, damaging your brand in the process.

Beyond you providing correct answers, they need to *believe* that you did. This means communicating with confidence. Providing the right answer only to have the caller dismiss it is only a slight improvement over providing the wrong answer.

Minimize Delays: Given the nature of call center work, it's not possible to have an agent answer every call on the first ring and never place the patient on hold. Yet you should strive to minimize service delays for those who contact you. This will do much to improve the patient experience.

This necessitates answering calls as quickly as possible. To truly count in callers' minds, this means being answered by a real person, not a recording. Having a computer answer their call accomplishes little, except when automated solutions can fully address the reason for their call or truly speed up their quest. But guess what? Though automated solutions may address some caller questions, seldom do they provide a full resolution.

Beyond answering quickly is minimizing hold time. In this regard, it doesn't matter how the call was put on hold. They don't care if they're listening to on-hold music because a machine put them there or if a person did it. They're still waiting. And they're growing increasingly discontent as each second ticks by.

A nice customer-friendly solution is to offer them the opportunity to receive a callback. Just make sure you follow through. If you don't, they'll call again, fuming as they wait to talk to your agent.

Offer Empathy: Medical call center agents handle the same types of calls all day long, day after day. They all too easily fall into a rut of moving from caller to caller with mechanical precision and detached emotion.

What is routine to them, however, is real and raw to the patient. What doesn't strike agents as urgent may loom as an emergency to the caller. Treat it as such.

Agents should never forget the perspective of their callers, making sure to offer empathy and compassion for the patient's situation. This may be the one hundredth such call for the agent, but it's the first one for the caller. Never lose sight of this as you seek to improve the patient experience.

Adopt a Patient-Centric Perspective: Though you don't want to disregard common call center metrics, adopt a patient-centric perspective.

Strive to provide correct answers, minimize delays, and offer empathy. If you do these three things, you'll be far ahead of most every other medical call center. Your patients will appreciate it—even if they never tell you.

Call Center Rx: Keep patients' needs and goals central to all that you do.

47. LESSEN PATIENT FRUSTRATION
CONSIDER THE CRITICAL ROLE OF MEDICAL ANSWERING SERVICES

Talk to just about anyone today about healthcare and they'll voice frustrations. Providers are frustrated that they're hampered from giving the best care to patients.

Patients are frustrated with the complexities of navigating the healthcare system and receiving the care they seek. They especially balk at automation that strives to save costs but does so at the expense of personal interaction and what patients want.

All, however, is not lost. The venerable medical answering service can help alleviate this frustration and increase patient satisfaction in ways that have been proven over time.

Always Available: Medical answering services operate 24/7. They never close. This means they provide around-the-clock telephone coverage. This includes daytime and evenings; weekdays and weekends; and even holidays—especially holidays.

Given this, when patients have a healthcare concern, they can talk to a real person at any time of the day or night. This fosters patient satisfaction.

People listen. Technology can't—not really.

People can ease frustrations. Technology causes angst more often than not. '

Offer Compassion: Another thing people can do that technology can't is to offer empathy. When we're hurting, we want to be heard. A little bit of sympathy goes a long way when we're not feeling well or have a healthcare concern.

Though technology has the potential to mimic compassion, it usually comes across as disingenuous. But this is where people shine. The medical answering service—staffed by real people—excels at offering compassion and being sympathetic to the plight of patients when they call.

Provide Solutions: Medical answering services can do more than process phone calls. They can also help address certain patient requests.

Consider, for example, appointments. When the medical answering service is connected to a doctor's scheduling system, they can set, change, and reschedule appointments. This serves patients better and saves the practice's office from dealing with scheduling issues.

Another example would be to transfer callers with health concerns to a telephone triage center. If telephone triage is not an option, medical answering services can screen calls—according to doctors' protocols—and reach the on-call doctor for issues that can't wait for the office to open.

Don't dismiss the respected medical answering service in a misguided effort to save money.

Call Center Rx: Embrace medical answering services to help doctors shine, increase patient satisfaction, and reduce the frustrations of all.

48. ENHANCE PATIENT SATISFACTION

THINK LIKE A CALLER AND NOT LIKE A CALL CENTER MANAGER

In healthcare we talk about the needs of patients, and in call centers we talk about the needs of callers, that is, patients who call on the phone.

Remove your call center manager hat for a moment and adopt the patient perspective of someone about to call with a question, problem, or complaint. It will take time you may feel you don't have but make time to do so. Encourage your agents to do the same thing.

Patients expect certain things when they call. Here are some ideas for enhancing patient satisfaction as you meet those expectations.

Be Nice: Call center agents are there to serve callers. The focus is service. Therefore, serve with a smile. Callers will hear it, even though they can't see it. Though it might be the fiftieth call that day for the agent, it's likely the first call for the patient. So be nice to them. They deserve it.

Seek a balance of being professional and being personable. Too professional comes across as distant, cold, and uncaring. Too personable comes across as sloppy, nonchalant, and unskilled.

Real professionalism implies competence, while true personality inspires approachability. Smartly combining them will improve patient satisfaction.

Respect Their Time: Patients want a quick resolution to their call. They'll say they want you to answer quickly, not transfer them, or put them on hold. That is, don't waste their time.

Though you can't answer every call on the first ring—nor should you—strive to find that right balance between optimum call center efficiency and ideal caller responsiveness. Their wait time should be minimal.

If they're in queue, let them know the projected wait time. Offer them the courtesy of a callback. Then make sure you do it.

But don't be in a rush either. Speed creates errors, which produces return calls and generates more work and needless activity. Take the time needed to do it right the first time. In doing so you'll enhance patient satisfaction.

Offer Correct Answers They Can Trust: Mostly, patients want to receive the right answer when they call. By the time they say goodbye, they should have confidence that they received the correct answer.

There are two elements here: the correct answer and a feeling of confidence.

Some agents give the right answer but fail to instill confidence in the caller. The patient doubts the information they received, even though it was correct. They'll likely call again to voice the same concern.

Other agents give the wrong answer but do so with such confidence that the caller doesn't realize they were misled until much later. The patient has already given a glowing response on your customer satisfaction survey but wishes they could take it back.

A few agents give the wrong answer, and the caller knows it.

The goal is to give the right answer and leave the caller feeling confident in the response. This is a win for everyone.

The agent appropriately serves the caller. The patient doesn't need to make a follow-up call. The call center saves time by avoiding unnecessary rework. And the patient saves their time too.

Call Center Rx: To improve patient satisfaction, be nice, respect their time, and offer correct answers they can trust.

49. GO BEYOND THE CALL
SEEK WAYS TO SOLVE CALLERS' PAIN POINTS

As a medical call center, your job is to answer healthcare-related calls and respond to each one efficiently. Yet what if this isn't what the patient needs? To paraphrase an old saying, sometimes you can win the battle but lose the war. That's why you need to go beyond the call.

Being efficient sometimes gets in the way of truly winning. Call centers have a lot of metrics to track. These help quantify results, but they may not measure outcomes. You need to find a balance between efficiency and patient-centric results.

Here are some ideas:

Sympathetic Listening: Sometimes callers need to know you heard them just as much as they need their issue addressed. This requires listening and offering empathy. Correcting a caller's issue but doing so abruptly or without listening to them leaves the caller more frustrated than satisfied.

To you, they are one more call in a busy shift. But to them you may be the most important call they'll make all day.

Pursue Resolution: Other times what a patient asks for isn't what they need—not really. Yet a passive-aggressive response results in answering the question, while not resolving the problem.

For example, a patient might ask for the web address of your online portal so they can check the results of a recent test. You give them the address because that's what they asked for. Yet you know the results they want won't be available for at least another day. Do you tell them that, even though it's not what they asked? Can you suggest a different method for them to get the results quicker?

Anticipate Problems: Let's say a patient calls to verify the location of where they need to go for an appointment with a specialist. You give them the address.

They didn't ask about parking, but you know that's an issue that frustrates many people. So, you can go the extra mile and let them know where they should park and how much time to allow themselves so they can arrive at the specialist's office without being frazzled or out of breath.

Stay on the Line: Back to the caller who asked for the web address. You can give it to them and get off the call. Or you can give it to them and stay on the line to see if they have any more questions. Maybe they entered it wrong. If you're still connected, you can clarify it, instead of making them call back a second time.

Or you can help them navigate the site, offering a quick tip that will save several minutes of frustration on their part. The point is, don't end the call prematurely. If you think they'll need help, the best approach may be to stick around.

Putting These Tips into Practice: You may acknowledge that while these are insightful ideas, they're not practical for your busy call center and that you can't afford to implement them. But recall the concept of winning the battle and losing the war.

That means the better perspective is that perhaps y you can't afford not to implement them. Think about it.

Call Center Rx: Look for ways to go the extra mile for patients. Encourage your staff to do the same.

50. PROVIDE MULTICHANNEL ACCESS
OFFER THE OPTIONS TODAY'S CONSUMERS EXPECT

We've talked about the need—either in concept or in reality—for medical call centers to become contact centers. This realignment shifts our attention from just telephone calls to embrace other forms of contact.

This is a multichannel mindset, and you provide multichannel access to deliver the contact options that today's consumers expect, which you must do if you're to remain accessible.

Some people call this omnichannel, which means *all* channels, while multichannel more realistically looks at *many* channels. We'll not debate which name is more appropriate. Instead, we'll focus on the concept of moving beyond the telephone.

Here are some multichannel access points to consider:

Telephone: The telephone remains key for most people in most industries. In the push for multichannel access, let's not forget phones. They will continue to be the foundation for what you do.

The telephone has been around for a long time, longer than any of us. The first medical call centers started a century ago in the form of medical answering services, sometimes called doctors' exchanges.

The telephone is proven, ubiquitous, and dependable. It's not new or exciting, but it is stable. And most consumers expect you to answer their phone calls.

Email: Email has been around for several decades. It's no longer novel, with naysayers long claiming that email is dead. It's not. It's very much alive. When you consider growing your call center beyond the telephone, the first multichannel access option to consider may be email.

Email integrates smartly into call center activity. Unlike the telephone, where callers expect a timely answer with minimal delay, their expectation with email is less demanding. This provides the opportunity to set email aside for a while when call traffic is high and to process email messages during slower times.

This doesn't mean you can sit on a pending email message for days. Instead, aim for a same-day response, which most people accept as a reasonable delay. Even so, providing a response within a couple of hours is better.

Email agents should be able to read and absorb typed information quickly. They should also be able to type fast and accurately, without the need for editing.

Text: A third multichannel access option to consider is text. This common, and increasingly popular, communication option is how many people communicate with their family and friends. It's no wonder that they expect businesses—including the healthcare industry—to embrace it too.

Text agents, like email agents, must be able to quickly process typed messages and respond with accuracy. Unlike email, however, texting carries with it the expectation of minimal delay. In comparing chat with telephone calls, where multitasking doesn't work, experienced chat agents can effectively handle multiple simultaneous chat sessions.

Social Media: Next consider social media. If patients try to contact you on social media, be prepared to respond. If you ignore them or take too long, they'll be sure to vent their frustration to everyone on their platform of choice.

Social media agents need many of the same skills as email and text agents. In addition, they must understand and be comfortable using each of the social media platforms that people could use to contact you.

Other Channels: This list is a great start, but it's not exclusive. If people want to contact you by mail or even fax, be ready to handle those interactions. Also watch for emerging communication technologies so you can prepare for them before your patients ask.

Implementation: If your call center is already providing multichannel access, that's great. Look for ways to make your channel offerings more effective.

And if your call center focuses exclusively on the phone, explore how you can move decisively and methodically forward to offer multichannel access to your patients and customers.

Call Center Rx: Move to a multichannel mindset in your call center.

51. TIPS TO DEAL WITH ANGRY PATIENTS
PREPARE HOW TO BEST HANDLE ABUSIVE CALLERS

It seems people today are more demanding and less tolerant than they once were. They want immediate answers and have little willingness to wait.

This unfortunate trend may be even more pronounced when speaking to someone over the telephone. This is the reality of angry callers that your medical call centers must deal with.

Here are some strategies to address this troubling issue.

Tips For Management

Determining an appropriate response to angry callers starts with call center leadership. Implement these ideas for your call center or organization to support your frontline people when they encounter a difficult phone call.

Have a Plan: Develop a written strategy for how agents should best respond to and deal with angry callers. This goes beyond nice-sounding platitudes and should offer practical, actionable steps. Provide recommendations for how agents should react to volatile callers and the options you recommend for them to best deal with the aftermath.

Communicate the Plan: Share your strategy with your staff.

Teach it during their initial training, reinforce it in ongoing instruction, and make it readily available to all parties: your frontline staff, your supervisors, and your managers.

Support Your Team: Let your staff know that you care how they're treated. The oft-repeated adage that "the customer is always right" isn't always true. Sometimes callers are wrong, unreasonable, or even mean. Let your agents know you're on their side.

Offer Options: In most instances, when an agent hangs up from one phone call, there's another one waiting in queue. The goal, in normal situations, is for the agent to immediately go to the next call. But after an extremely difficult interaction, they may not be at their best to assist the next caller right away.

Give them options to take after draining interactions or else they risk turning one bad call into a string of bad calls. One idea is allowing them to take themselves out of rotation for a moment to regain their composure. Extreme cases may warrant taking an early break. Just place appropriate guidelines on when these steps are applicable.

Tips For Agents

I hope your call center has provided instruction and tools to help you deal with angry callers who won't calm down. Always follow their policy.

But if you're in a position without the needed direction, here are some ideas you can use to better cope with abusive callers. Exercise care, however, to use these sparingly, especially as you move down the list.

Also, your organization may have given you variations on these techniques, so follow their processes. Don't be alarmed if your call center prohibits one or more of these options, particularly the last one. Know that they have a good reason for doing so. Respect it and follow their wishes.

Lower Your Voice: It's in our nature to raise our voice in response to someone who raises theirs. This just escalates the situation. Instead, do the opposite. Talk more softly. They're apt to do the same. And even if they don't, it will calm you.

Take Five: Sometimes a five-second respite at the conclusion of a phone call can help. Close your eyes, inhale slowly, exhale slowly, and quiet your emotions. Do a shoulder roll to release tension.

Press Hold: When a caller escalates out of control, place them on hold under the guise of needing to check something. Maybe you actually do, and you'll be able to accomplish it more effectively if they aren't venting their anger in the process.

But even if you don't need to check something, use this time to refocus yourself. Hopefully, they'll calm down a bit as well. Just make sure you politely and patiently explain to them that you will place them on hold before pressing that button.

Pass Off the Call: Do you have a supervisor or manager who can help you deal with difficult callers?

Sometimes your coworker sitting next to you can serve as an ad hoc "supervisor" to take a difficult caller that you're not connecting with. Of course, be willing to do the same when they have a difficult conversation of their own.

Know That It's Not Personal: Most angry callers are mad at your organization, and they take it out on you as its representative. Know that their frustration isn't personally directed at you. This understanding puts a buffer between their emotions and your self-esteem.

Though this is easier to say than to do, acknowledging that their anger isn't personal may help you take an emotional step back from a volatile situation.

But Sometimes It Is Personal: Occasionally, however, an angry caller becomes abusive and attacks you personally. They may call you a name, question your intelligence, or worse. These direct attacks sting. It becomes personal.

You can't separate yourself from their emotion because they just verbally assaulted you. If this occurs and none of the above options help, you're justified in telling the caller their behavior is inappropriate. Explain that you want to help, but until they calm down you won't be able to.

If they persist, warn them that you'll need to disconnect their call. If they refuse to soften their demeanor, hang up.

Call Center Rx: Though you can do little to change how abusive callers treat you, you can control how you respond.

52. UPSELL FUTILITY
WOULD YOU LIKE FRIES WITH THAT?

I needed to order some ink cartridges for my printer, the kind I can only buy from the vendor. Here's what happened and the lessons we can learn from it.

Five Upsell Attempts: I called and told the agent I wanted to order two black ink cartridges. Not surprisingly, she suggested I buy a package that included two color cartridges. "No thank you, just black," I replied.

Upon discovering the age of my printer (only eighteen months), she tried to sell me a new one. "No thank you. I just need ink."

When I acknowledged that I own several computers from her company, she asked, "Are they working okay? Do you want to—"

"No, I just want to buy ink."

Then she offered me a special price on anti-virus software for only . . .

"No, I only want ink!"

Next, she inquired if I was interested in a maintenance plan to . . .

"NO, just ink!"

Perhaps she was supposed to try to upsell me five times, or maybe she was on commission. I don't know, but I do know the call took much longer than necessary. I became irritated, and I won't buy another printer from this vendor.

A Healthcare Parallel: Now let's imagine a call to refill my prescription. The agent says, "Would you like to meet with the doctor to review your current health status?"

I decline.

"When was your last annual checkup? Should I schedule you for one?"

I refuse.

"We have a special this month on colonoscopies, and I see you're at the age . . ."

I spurn that offer.

"Can I have a representative contact you to review all the services we offer?"

I reject her offer.

"We have a new family plan to save—"

"NO!"

What would be the result of this pretend health call? Did we have a positive interaction? Has the agent made a positive impression? The next time I have a healthcare need, will this organization be the first on my list to contact—or the last?

Call Center Rx: Be sure any upsell initiatives don't irritate patients and drive them away.

53. AN ER VISIT IS MORE THAN GREAT CARE
DON'T OVERLOOK GREAT FOLLOW-UP

I once took a trip to the ER as a patient. It was for one of those silly things; I guess that's why they call them accidents. A series of small decisions throughout my day resulted in a final "oops" at the wrong time and . . . well, I'll spare you the details.

My wife drove while I applied pressure to my hand. The ER was empty (great timing on my part), so we were in and out quickly. Ninety minutes later I was back home, doted upon by my sympathetic wife.

Great Care: From a customer service standpoint, the ER staff did everything right. They were personable, empathetic, efficient, supportive, and effective. I bantered with the nurse and complimented the doctor as she stitched me up (six, if you're interested). They gave me detailed discharge instructions, answered my questions, and listened as I recapped what I understood them to say.

I expected the proverbial icing on the cake the next day with a follow-up phone call. The call never came. I wish it had, because by then I had another question.

Eight days later I returned to have my stitches removed. To my delight, I saw the same nurse and the same doctor. Everything looked good; the scarring would be minimal. I was in and out in a few minutes.

No Follow-Up: Would I receive a phone call this time? Nope.

They could have called (or emailed, or snail-mailed): "Thank you for using our services; we know you have options in healthcare and appreciate you picking us."

They also could have called to connect me with a primary care physician, since I confessed to not currently having one when they admitted me. What a great way to keep me in their system and do more business with me in the future.

They missed two opportunities: one to better serve me then and another to ensure my future patronage. What a difference just one phone call could have made.

Call Center Rx: Don't forget the value of a timely follow-up call after an ER visit or other significant interaction.

TOOLS

54. KEY REASONS TO IMPLEMENT NEW TECHNOLOGY
NOW IS THE TIME TO INVEST IN YOUR CALL CENTER'S FUTURE

Long gone are the days when all you needed was a telephone and a message pad to handle phone calls. For decades, call centers have relied on technology to increase efficiency and optimize results. And never has that been truer than today.

Consider these four reasons to invest in call center technology.

You Can Save Time and Increase Efficiency: Advanced technology can offer time-saving processes that will increase the efficiency of your staff. This means they can do more work in the same time or the same work in less time.

In these instances, you can perform an analysis to calculate your payback period. This is a great approach to cost-justify a technology investment.

You Can Provide Additional Services: Older equipment can limit the services you provide, but an upgrade may allow you to increase the scope of what you offer to your patients or callers. Again, you can calculate the payback period of your investment.

You Can Go Online: Many older systems are premise-based, making it difficult to have a distributed workforce or to establish remote work sessions. The interest and the need for people to work at home will never go away, which has accelerated the trend toward home-based solutions. Your future may depend on having this flexibility, so make the move today to prepare for tomorrow.

You Can Avoid Obsolescence: A final consideration is platform age. Sometimes you take a system as far as it will let you, and then it limits the service you provide to callers. If you're trying to operate using out-of-date technology, you may not be able to cost-justify the investment by calculating the payback period. But that doesn't remove the fact that replacing an obsolete system is an essential move if you want to remain a viable resource for your organization and callers.

Looking Forward: Your call center may already have the best technology available. But remember that systems are always changing, and what's best today won't be the best tomorrow. Most call centers, however, have a platform with at least a few areas that need improving. Now is the time to plan to make that happen.

Call Center Rx: Though you don't always need the latest technology, make sure your systems aren't hampering what you do.

55. WILL TEXT REPLACE THE TELEPHONE?

BALANCE OLD TECHNOLOGIES WITH NEW

With the younger generation's love for texting and their general avoidance of placing a phone call, it's tempting to project the demise of the call center. Although this may make for a logical conclusion, it's not going to happen in the foreseeable future. Though tomorrow's medical call center will undoubtedly have more chat transactions than it does now, the telephone will remain its primary communication device.

Why?

The reason is the simple fact that calls are superior in several key situations, and these significant advantages will not go away any time soon.

Talking Is More Effective: Speaking is faster than typing. When describing complex medical situations, saying our words is more effective than keying them. With the status of our health at stake, we want to communicate quickly and get it right the first time. The telephone allows us to do this.

Our Tone Carries Meaning: Emotions are more easily understood when they're communicated verbally. Humor, desperation, and pain do not come across well in written form. How many times have you had a text message or email be misunderstood because your tone of voice didn't come across as you intended?

Likewise, healthcare provider empathy comes across better when talking, instead of typing. It's hard to communicate compassion in nonwritten forms. Yes, we do have emojis, but they're prone to misunderstandings too.

People Pick Up the Phone: In stressful situations, people of all generations will gravitate to the phone. It provides for fast and efficient communication in time-critical, stressful situations, such as when reaching out for medical help. The telephone offers a simple, no-hassle way to communicate. That's why it's the go-to tool for difficult situations.

Yes, texting is the newer technology that is growing in use and popularity, while the telephone seems stodgy and old school in comparison. Yet when critical, timely, and accurate communication is essential, the telephone wins almost every time.

In the future, your medical call center will undoubtedly handle more texting. The telephone, however, will continue to ring for many situations.

To prepare for the future, embrace chat technology, if you haven't already done so. But don't lose sight of the telephone. It will continue to be a critical part of your medical call center operation for many years to come.

Call Center Rx: As you embrace texting, don't dismiss the telephone.

56. REVIEW YOUR WEBSITE
EVALUATE YOUR ONLINE INFORMATION AND MAKE SURE IT'S UP TO DATE

For the past 25 years I've worked on my own websites, designing them, posting content, and keeping them up to date. Sometimes I break them too; then I get to fix my mistakes.

At my peak, I had ten websites for myself, my writing, and my businesses. Though this experience doesn't make me a website guru, it has taught me to look at the sites I visit with a critical eye.

Sadly, I see areas that need improvement on most websites. And too many have obsolete information. You probably know your website needs some attention, but you haven't gotten around to doing it.

I urge you to move this task from your want-to-do list and put it into your schedule. Write it down and put a date on it. Then do it. Here are some things to consider:

Read Through Your Website: Start by going through your website. Read through your site methodically, page by page, and read every one. Unless you want to be extra diligent, you can skip blog posts. The main thing is to focus on the pages.

This is hard to do and time-consuming, especially for large sites. It's something I don't do often enough myself, but don't follow my example. You can do better; after all, you probably don't have ten sites to go through.

To get through it faster, you can always ask for other people in your organization to help. This will make the job go faster and be less taxing for everyone.

As you read each page, look for out-of-date text and missing information. Also be on the lookout for missing words, wrong words, and punctuation errors. Likewise flag confusing information so you can fix it later.

Pages to Remove: As you go through your site, you may come across pages you don't need anymore. Make a note to remove those obsolete pages. The good news is that once you decide you don't need it, you can stop reading it.

Pages to Add: Just as there are pages you may want to remove, you'll also discover important content that's missing. Make a note to add it. This may include new services or products, procedural changes, and information your patients or visitors may commonly seek.

For ideas, check with your call center agents to find out what questions they keep hearing over and over. This is prime material to go online. Yes, not everyone will see it, and they'll still call and ask. But some people will notice it, and then you've just saved your staff a needless phone call.

Site Navigation: When it comes to adding new pages and removing obsolete ones, this affects your website menu and site navigation. You need to adjust your menu accordingly.

Don't just add or delete options. Instead, take a step back and see if the navigation is logical, intuitive, and easy to use. For help, ask someone outside your organization to look at it and tell you what confuses them about navigating it. Then implement their suggestions.

Call Center Rx: Review your website to ensure it provides correct information and gives visitors what they're looking for.

57. DO VIDEO CALLS HAVE A PLACE IN YOUR CONTACT CENTER?
EXAMINE THE BENEFITS AND DISADVANTAGES OF VIDEO CALLING

For years, some call center managers have anticipated having video capability in their call centers. Others weren't so open to the idea. And most agents have opposed it as well.

Yet the past few years have prepared us, even conditioned us, to participate in video communication. If you don't have video in your call center, now might be the right time to explore it more seriously.

The Benefits of Video: There are three components to our communication: words, tone, and nonverbal. The words we use comprise only 7 percent of our communication. Our tone of voice and inflection account for another 38 percent. The remaining 55 percent is nonverbal; it's our body language.

In a call center, agents can only use words and vocal components to communicate with callers. This totals 45 percent, with agents not being able to tap into the remaining 55 percent nonverbal component.

Video calls add this nonverbal component into the mix, allowing for 100 percent of communication to occur. The result is enhanced interaction, more effective information exchange, and easier rapport building. These combine to improve customer service, which results in happier callers, less miscommunication, and fewer callbacks.

An added benefit in the healthcare industry is the ability to see patients online, which can be a huge benefit, especially in telephone triage.

The Disadvantages of Video: Despite all the upsides to video calls, there are some downsides as well.

Employees opt for call center work for assorted reasons. A common one is that they want to avoid in-person interaction with the public. This may be due to appearance, low self-confidence, or social anxiety. They feel safe and competent over the phone, whereas they would struggle with in-person scenarios. Adding video to the call center removes this safety net.

Other agents may feel uncomfortable in front of the camera, not have a personality that works with video, or lack the presence needed for successful visual communication.

In these situations, forcing an employee to accept video as part of their work may alienate them, decrease their work effectiveness, or cause them to resign.

Preparing for Video Calls: Here are some tips to successfully implement video in your call center:

- **Make it optional for existing employees**: Allow them to opt out if they're uncomfortable. Don't penalize them for this.
- **Provide training**: Though most employees know how to use a camera—from both a technical and practical standpoint—not all will. Offer instruction as needed.
- **Review your dress code**: Some call centers have a relaxed dress code or no dress code, reasoning that when you're talking on the phone it doesn't matter what you look like. This goes away with video. Make sure video agents look presentable.
- **Update your documentation**: Verify that your employee handbook, policies, and written expectations reflect video calling and the use of cameras in your call center.

- **Hire new employees for video**: Screen applicants and hire staff with the expectation of video.

With these elements in place, you're ready to move forward with video calls in your contact center. May you enjoy the process and realize success.

Call Center Rx: Be open to have video calling as a part of your call center.

58. INTEGRATE YOUR CALL CENTER TOOLS

MAKE SURE EACH PIECE OF TECHNOLOGY WORKS AS PART OF A SEAMLESS SYSTEM

Today's vendors offer a wide array of technology options to enhance the contact center operation. Yet if these tools don't integrate with each other, you lose—or even negate—their promised productivity outcomes.

Having technology tools that won't talk with one another is almost as detrimental as not having the tools in the first place. Therefore, it's essential that you integrate your contact center's tools and technology.

Here are some key considerations:

Interoperability: We've all called places and given basic information in step one of the contact, only to have to repeat it in step two. This happens too often, and it infuriates callers, setting the stage for ineffective communications from the onset. I've had many instances where I had to repeat the same information multiple times. One company made me reconfirm my identity each time they transferred my call.

Today's consumers—your healthcare system's patients and customers—deserve better and expect more. Complete integration passes on all collected information through each step of the call.

This includes transfers, switching channels, and moving between systems.

Databases: Today's healthcare providers amass a plethora of information. This data ends up in a database, but usually it's not just one and often several. Too often inter-database integration is nonexistent. Even a basic interface is missing.

This requires contact center agents and healthcare professionals to reenter information, transferring it from one source to another.

Sometimes this requires rekeying, which is time-consuming and error prone. Even copy-and-paste functionality fails to provide the desired ease of information transfer.

Then, with the same information existing in two places, a nonintegrated environment means that updates must also occur in two—or more—places. This seldom happens and points to the need to better integrate call center tools.

I know this from experience. I've had organizations try to call me on a number I cancelled years prior. Though I let them know of the change when I moved, not every record received the update. Hence needless frustration on their part and mine.

Apps: Similar to databases are apps and software. Though on a basic level this is addressed with interoperability initiatives and database integration, more work still needs to be done.

Many times I've had reps tell me they were writing down the information I gave them so they wouldn't have to have me repeat it as they moved from one program to another.

I've also had instances where they didn't write down what I gave them, but they tried to remember it. And they remembered it wrong. This meant I had to correct them and give the same information again.

Does your message taking app integrate with your appointment setting app? Does your answering service software integrate with your telephone triage software? Does your class scheduling program interface with your literature request program?

Call Center Rx: To provide a holistic and satisfying solution to patients, fully integrate your call center tools to optimize your operation.

59. MULTICHANNEL INTEGRATION
SERVE PATIENTS BETTER AND PRODUCE SUPERIOR OUTCOMES

Some medical call centers only handle telephone calls by design and others do it because that's what they've always done. But most have embraced a *contact* center mindset, where they handle more than just phone calls.

Channel Options: Moving beyond the telephone can include email, text messaging, and chat. It may also incorporate social media monitoring and response.

There is also an opportunity with video. Integrating video communications into the call center has received much theoretical attention for a couple of decades, with proponents predicting it would be only a year or two out. We are, at last, moving from potential to possible.

Over the past few years many people have become more comfortable using a camera to communicate with someone far away. Though not everyone embraced this as an acceptable alternative to in-person meetings, they did, however, become more comfortable using it and less resistant to the technology.

This prepares people for the option of video chatting with their healthcare provider, nurse triage operation, or medical answering service. These are exciting times for patients and their medical call centers.

Channel Switching: All these options, however, will inevitably lead to patients using multiple communication channels to accomplish their task, depending on what's available at the time or what will achieve their goal the fastest.

What could start as a telephone call could switch to video for face-to-face interaction. In the same way, a text message chain could migrate to the telephone, or a social media post could lead to email.

Multichannel Integration: Yet regardless of the scenario, one key issue remains paramount. Each channel must integrate with all the others, allowing information to effortlessly pass from one option to another. You must eliminate isolated silos of information that don't communicate with each other. You need full multichannel integration.

This usually falls to the platform vendor. If you use a singular system to handle all communication channels, you're one step closer to making multichannel integration a reality. Though harder, integration between disparate systems can also occur. It just requires more effort on the part of the respective vendors to pull off.

Here's what you can do to move things forward to enjoy multichannel integration.

Educate Staff: Make sure your front-line employees know what they must do to allow for the smoothest information handoff as patients move from one channel to another. If your staff doesn't do their part correctly, the degree of integration won't matter.

Test Your System: Make a contact on one channel as a patient would. Then switch channels and see what happens. Is your text messaging exchange accessible by the telephone rep when you switch to voice? Or do you need to start over and re-state the same information?

Test this in each combination of channels possible. Regardless of how unlikely it seems to you that anyone would ever make that switch, know that someone will.

Identify Weaknesses: As you conduct your field tests of switching channels, look for three things. Identify what works well, what somewhat works, and what doesn't work at all. Celebrate the areas of success, seek ways to shore up limitations, and try to fix what doesn't work at all.

Encourage Your Vendor: Armed with this information, approach your vendor, not in a confrontational manner, but with a positive, let's-work-together attitude to move toward full multi-channel integration.

Call Center Rx: Multichannel integration is what your patients expect and deserve.

60. REMOTE PATIENT MONITORING
ADD NEW SERVICES TO BETTER SERVE YOUR STAKEHOLDERS

Whether you're an in-house medical call center provider or a for-profit outsourcer, look for ways to add more services to better serve your stakeholders. This will increase your value to them and help your community. It will also increase the value of your operation to your organization or to owners.

One such option is remote patient monitoring.

The Situation: Remote patient monitoring tracks the output of patient devices as they gather healthcare-related data. Much of this plethora of information yields to automation. But at some point, the output requires human intervention. Why not let your call center agents provide that first level of personal evaluation that surpasses an algorithm or exceeds the abilities of artificial intelligence (AI).

You already have the staff to do it. Regardless of if they have medical training or not, they do have a working understanding of healthcare. For those who lack the needed credentials, they can follow the protocols established by healthcare professionals.

You also have the essential infrastructure in place. Though you may need to add a module or app to your existing platform to handle remote patient monitoring, you already have the basic technology in your call center.

The Benefits: When you offer remote patient monitoring, two benefits result.

The first one is that you can better serve your stakeholders and the medical community. And the other outcome is that you make yourself a more valuable resource.

If you're an in-house operation, this earns you more attention at budget time and increased esteem within your organization. And if you're an outsource call center, the results are increased revenues and a more holistic service package to offer to your clients.

The Plan: Don't rush into remote patient monitoring without careful forethought. Consider the technology requirements, the training portion, and the legal aspect. None of these are insurmountable issues, but it's critical to address each one in advance. As the adage goes, an ounce of prevention is worth a pound of cure.

By all means, investigate remote patient monitoring for your medical call center. If you proceed, just make sure you do it right.

Call Center Rx: Consider if your call center should offer remote patient monitoring.

MOVING FORWARD

We've now covered sixty topics relevant to medical call centers. Along with them we offered sixty prescriptions: encouragements or ideas for action. Although not every item applies to every situation, most will.

Regardless of where you're at, know that for this book to be anything more than a thought-provoking read, you must respond. Now is the time for action. This doesn't mean all sixty items. It could be just one—for now. The key is to plan and then work your plan.

Do you already have your to-do list started? That's great!

Or is your mind spinning with ideas? Perhaps you're overwhelmed. If so, don't despair. Go through this book again to see what clicks and what doesn't apply.

As you do, the first step is to make a list of possible action items. Don't evaluate them just yet. Once you have your list, now it's time to prioritize them. Look for the items that are the most essential and will have the greatest impact. Treat it like a triage for your call center.

If it helps, our sixty prescriptions are summarized on the following pages.

Regardless of how you decide to proceed, let this book guide you in moving forward. You can do it. Start today.

Call Center Rx Summary
Leadership

1. Whatever channels your contact center covers, keep in mind that it's not about the technology, it's about the contact.
2. Strive to staff your multichannel contact center with both channel specialists and generalists.
3. Tap lessons from online and in-person communications to enhance your call center operation and boost agent effectiveness.
4. Guide your staff to embrace change and move toward establishing a change-oriented culture.
5. If you don't prepare for the future, the future will control you.
6. Determine the appropriate hourly rate for your agents to distinguish your compensation and expectations from competing employers.
7. True work-life balance may be an illusion you'll never reach, but that doesn't mean you shouldn't try to get closer to it.
8. Show each caller just how important they are by how you treat them and how you serve them.
9. Strive to work with the marketing department, not in opposition.
10. Do what you can today to best prepare for tomorrow. Don't put off until next year what you can finish now.

Management

11. Embrace call center metrics as a tool to help you manage more effectively.
12. To best evaluate call center success, stop focusing on speed and start focusing on quality.
13. Eliminate unneeded procedures and streamline rules to make your agents' jobs easier.
14. Streamlining your processes saves time, reduces errors, and increases efficiency.
15. Embrace—or at least consider—the value of video in your call center.
16. Whether remote work is your new normal or a hoped-for one-time necessity, make sure your policies and procedures adequately cover it.
17. Look at the pros and cons to determine if having work-at-home agents is the right solution for your call center. Then factor in the risks.
18. Successful management of remote workers requires a shift in perspective and practice.
19. Pick one thing you can do now that will make the future better. Don't let the urgency of today keep you from addressing this important initiative.
20. You can't stop negative information from spreading over the internet, but you can mitigate its impact by forming a plan for how to best respond.

Agents

21. Look for more ways to celebrate your agents' achievements and trumpet their accomplishments.
22. Hire staff with the skills needed for today and anticipated for tomorrow.
23. When training agents, communicate expectations, reinforce fundamentals, and teach advanced customer service skills.

24. Cross-trained agents increase their value to your organization, patients and callers benefit, and contact center efficiency increases.
25. Pursue the cross-channel training strategy that's ideal for your operation, your patients, and your staff. Balance their needs to provide the best outcome for all stakeholders.
26. Take a methodical approach to scheduling agents in a multichannel contact center.
27. Don't accept agent burnout as inevitable. Strive to combat it.
28. Strive to move closer to realizing a happier and more effective workforce.
29. Look for ways to affirm your staff and the work they do.
30. To move forward with a positive attitude, remember the good calls and encouraging callers.
31. Remember how much you have to be thankful for. You have a job that provides for you, benefits society, and carries significance.

Quality

32. View training as an ongoing necessity.
33. To address call center quality, strive to please callers. That's what matters most.
34. Prove your claims about quality service by doing it.
35. Implement a QA program to celebrate agent success, let them self-identify areas for improvement, and enhance customer service.
36. Among the many benefits of outsourcing call center work is the potential to improve quality.

Perspective

37. Having others view your call center differently starts with you. Rebrand your operation.
38. Draft or update your call center's mission statement.
39. Look for ways to better embrace your stakeholders.
40. Seek to align with your organization by working together for your patients' good and not in opposition to it.
41. Pursue integration initiatives to make your call center operation more effective and be a nicer, saner place to work.
42. Strive to build a strong call center team.
43. To get the best results, you need to start with the best staff.
44. Increase the visibility of your call center within your organization. If you don't, you'll become invisible and soon be overlooked.
45. Increase call center work flexibility by decentralizing your agent deployment options.

Patients

46. Keep patients' needs and goals central to all that you do.
47. Embrace medical answering services to help doctors shine, increase patient satisfaction, and reduce the frustrations of all.
48. To improve patient satisfaction, be nice, respect their time, and offer correct answers they can trust.
49. Look for ways to go the extra mile for patients. Encourage your staff to do the same.
50. Move to a multichannel mindset in your call center.
51. Though you can do little to change how abusive callers treat you, you can control how you respond.
52. Be sure any upsell initiatives don't irritate patients and drive them away.
53. Don't forget the value of a timely follow-up call after an ER visit or other significant interaction.

Tools

54. Though you don't always need the latest technology, make sure your systems aren't hampering what you do.
55. As you embrace texting, don't dismiss the telephone.
56. Review your website to ensure it provides correct information and gives visitors what they're looking for.
57. Be open to have video calling as a part of your call center.
58. To provide a holistic and satisfying solution to patients, fully integrate your call center tools to optimize your operation.
59. Multichannel integration is what your patients expect and deserve.
60. Consider if your call center should offer remote patient monitoring.

ABOUT PETER LYLE DEHAAN

Peter Lyle DeHaan, PhD, is a call center veteran. His lifetime of experience includes leading and managing a multi-location call center, employment with an industry vendor, call center consulting, and publishing call center periodicals and books.

Learn more at PeterLyleDeHaan.com.

BOOKS BY PETER LYLE DEHAAN

Call Center Success Series

The Profitable Answering Service

Call Center Connections

Healthcare Call Center Essentials

How to Start a Telephone Answering Service

Sticky Success Strategies

Sticky Customer Service

Sticky Sales and Marketing

Sticky Leadership and Management

Sticky Living

Academic Research

The Telephone Answering Service Industry

Turning a Telephone Answering Service into a Call Center

Other Books

Successful Author FAQs

For a complete, up-to-date list of Peter's books, go to PeterLyleDeHaan.com/books.

www.ingramcontent.com/pod-product-compliance
Lightning Source LLC
LaVergne TN
LVHW021816060526
838201LV00058B/3407